PP/FF:
An Anthology

Edited by Peter Conners

Starcherone Books / Buffalo, NY

PP/FF:
An Anthology

Edited by Peter Conners

Starcherone Books, Buffalo, NY 14201
www.starcherone.com

Cover painting: Mark Lavatelli, *Spruce Posse #3*, 2004, oil and charcoal on canvas, 54"
x 66".
Cover design: Geoffrey Gatza
Layout: Kevin Thurston
Proofreading: Buffalo Soldiers

Permissions may be found at the end of the book.

Library of Congress Cataloging-in-Publication Data

PP/FF : an anthology / edited by Peter Conners.
    p. cm.
 Includes bibliographical references.
 ISBN-13: 978-0-9703165-1-6 (alk. paper)
 ISBN-10: 0-9703165-1-8 (alk. paper)
 1. American literature--21st century. 2. Prose poems, American. 3.
Short stories, American. I. Conners, Peter H. II. Title.

 PS536.3.P73 2006
 810.8'006--dc22

2006001904

Table of Contents

Introduction to PP/FF: An Anthology
Peter Conners

> *He not busy being born*
> *Is busy dying*
> -Bob Dylan

B etrand Mathieu has written extensively on the role of Orphism in the work of Arthur Rimbaud, Charles Baudelaire, and Blaise Cendrars. He seldom uses the term prose poetry and never flash fiction. These writers were less concerned with genre than with finding the right forms to communicate their particular physical, intellectual, and spiritual visions. We group them together because their forms are similar and their influences overlap. In American literary circles they have been primarily classified as prose poets. They did not give themselves that label. According to Mathieu, they are Orphic writers based on their following of literary, and often personal, structures of katabasis "descent" and palingenesis "ascent/rebirth." To many, the tale of Orpheus and Eurydice is a tragic love story. To these writers, Mathieu argues, it is a blueprint for literary structure. Not genre, but structure. A structure realized through lyrical (the lyre of Orpheus) narratives describing descents through quotidian reality to subterranean levels of consciousness and spirituality (the land of Hades) communicated through poetic movements of symbol and language.

No doubt there are writers today who are comfortable with the label prose poetry. Since the 1960s this has come to be the accepted classification for, as Michael Benedikt puts it, "A form of poetry self-consciously written in prose, yet characterized by the conscious, intense use, of virtually all the devices of verse poetry—except for strict meter; rhyme; and the line-break." Such acceptance comes with intellectual inquiry; to become a valid genre, writing with similar qualities must be grouped, studied, and quantified. To become a vital genre those quantifiable traits must be perpetuated. To grow stale, those traits must become so entrenched that deviation is regarded as radicalism, or worse, artistic failure.

In 2006, it is fair to say that prose poetry is a vital American genre: there are prose poetry journals, anthologies, university courses, and attendant experts. Perhaps classifying it as a stale genre is too harsh, however, in compiling this anthology it became obvious that many writers have felt shunned from traditional communities of poetry and prose—including prose poetry—for consciously resisting genre expectations. To wit, prose poetry should not contain too much narrative or it becomes fiction; flash fiction should follow a narrative arc or it risks fragmentation to the point of becoming prose poetry; flash fiction should stay within specific, albeit arbitrary, word counts; prose poetry must not utilize line break; surrealism and humor is acceptable, but topicality is not....

Based on Michael Benedikt's useful definition of prose poetry, and the generally accepted understanding that a flash fiction is a very short, traditionally structured story, it seems that these writers are at very least expanding the parameters of what constitutes a prose poem or a flash fiction. It is also true that some of their work is neither prose poem nor flash fiction. As a reader, writer, and editor it is my opinion that this "neither" type of writing is so contemporarily important as to define a zeitgeist. Thus PP/FF was created as a symbol by which we can discuss writing born of the spirit of our times. As I wrote in an essay that served as an introduction to the PP/FF issue of *American Book Review* (Vol. 26, No. 2): *PP/FF is meant as a label that locates the territory of prose poetry and flash fiction by symbol rather than by language prejudiced by old genre baggage. PP/FF is prose poetry and flash fiction balanced on a makeshift teeter-totter that never lands. Sometimes it is more prose poetry, sometimes more flash fiction, but it is always in motion between the two. PP/FF is a symbol of a vital and important literary form that is constantly in flux, appropriating, moving and growing.*

Conditioned by linear narrative tales, we optimistically expect our descents to breed ascent and satisfying conclusions. That is seldom the case. Narrative arc is also a myth: PP/FF has been uttered and must ascend and descend as it is needed. Perhaps the writers in this anthology will be thought of as PP/FF writers. Perhaps poets, fiction writers, or followers of Orpheus (After losing Eurydice, Orpheus turned away from the cult of Dionysus to preach the glory of Apollo causing an angry Dionysus to send his Maenads to tear Orpheus's body apart. Orpheus's head floated, still singing, down the Hebros River until it came to rest in a cave at Antissa where it served as a disembodied prophet. Eventually Apollo grew angry that his own oracle at Delphi was being neglected in favor of this oracle of Orpheus. Apollo silenced the head.). I created PP/FF as a symbol rather than a word in the hopes of breaking down the restrictions of genre. I have no interest in creating new confinements. Rather, I would argue that strict adherence to given definitions of form and genre (pre-fabricated marketing boxes), are debilitating to a writer's creativity and do a disservice to readers. Genre is easier to sell, to teach, to quantify and review, but what does it have to do with creating new art? The writing in this anthology resists definition and often challenges readers' assumptions about genre, form, style, and content. It entertains, but also demands that questions be asked. Each piece creates its own rules.

Peter Conners
Rochester, New York

References

Mathieu, Bertrand. *Orpheus in Brooklyn: Orphism, Rimbaud, and Henry Miller.* Gainsville, FL: Florida Academic Press, Inc, 2003.

Benedikt, Michael. "Michael Benedikt Talks About Prose Poetry." New York, NY: *PSA Newsletter* #19, 1985.

Remove it and there's sunlight. Terraced vineyards, a grove of olive trees, the netting of an old bridal gown shading the staked tomato plants, the sound of a distant accordion squeezed in time to the swish of the sea.

Remove it and it's as if you've lifted off the weight of memory. Memory that was once so companionable, and that now has turned into an assassin. Memory, with its offended honor, with its vendetta, giving you the evil eye like the godmother of a jilted bride. You work the razor along your throat while, veiled in dust, the bride stares back from a mirror that's framed in black like a sympathy card, an antique mirror whose fly spots have become freckles of age, whose spidery cracks and broken capillaries have reassembled into the image of your face juxtaposed upon her face, a mirror whose motto is "J'accuse."

Remove it and there's the tintentabulation of shells as the sea laps the sand. Crystalline blue water spattered by flying fish. A lemon grove in blossom. And beyond the bees, the sound of a river. And across the river on a distant bank of sunflowers, someone cupping a harmonica

But put it on and its brim of shadow extends until there's barely enough light to see the five stairs leading down to the wet street. Moon the backside of a mirror; streetlamps in tulle. And from a black framed doorway, exactly like the doorway you've stepped through, straightening his hat as you straighten yours, an assassin also descends five steps, pausing only to strike and cup a match. In the blue flare, you recognize the face as your face the same face imprinted on all you've come to kill.

Sister Francetta and the Pig Baby
Kenneth Bernard

L et me get right into it. When Sister Francetta was a little girl she looked into a baby carriage one day and saw a baby with a pig head. It wore dainty white clothes, had little baby hands and feet, a baby's body. Of course the sounds it made were strange, but the main thing was the pig head. It lay there on its back, kicking its feet, waving its arms, and staring at the world through a pig head. Now Sister Francetta taught us her morality through stories. For example, little boys and girls who put their fingers in forbidden places sometimes found that their fingers rotted away. That was the moral of a story about a boy who picked his nose. However, rotting fingers were a comparatively mild consequence. Sister Francetta's childhood world was filled with sudden and horrible attacks of blindness, deafness, and dumbness. Ugly purple growths developed overnight anywhere inside or outside of people's bodies. Strange mutilations from strange accidents were common. It absolutely did not pay to be bad. Sinful thoughts were the hardest to protect against. Prayer and confession were the surest remedies. As I grew older, Sister Francetta's tales gradually subsided into remote pockets of my mind, occasionally to crop up in dream or quaint reminiscence. Except for the pig baby. The pig baby is still with me. It was different from her other stories. For example, it had no moral, it was just there: there had once been a baby with a pig head. Also, whereas Sister Francetta told her other stories often, and with variations, she told the story of the pig baby only once. And she told it differently, as if she herself did not understand it but nevertheless felt a tremendous urgency to reveal it. The other stories she told because they were *useful*. The story of the pig baby she told because she had *faith* in it. It captured my imagination totally. I tried to find out more, but she usually put me off. And I thought a great deal about it. Since Sister Francetta is dead now, I suppose I am the only expert in the world on the pig baby, and what I know can be listed very quickly:

1. The pig baby was apparently Caucasian.
2. Its parents were proud of it and in public seemed totally unaware of its pig head.
3. I do not know how long it lived. It apparently never went to school.
4. It always snorted noticeably but never let out any really piglike sounds like *oink*.
5. It ate and drank everything a regular baby ate and drank.
6. Its parents were not Catholic.
7. Everyone pretended not to notice that the baby had a pig head. For some reason it was not talked about either.
8. At some early point the family either moved away or disappeared.
9. No one said anything about that either.

Sister Francetta died a few years after I had her as a teacher. She was still young. It was whispered among us that she had horrible sores all over her body. I became an excellent student and went on to college. There I developed more sophisticated ideas about the pig baby, the two most prominent of which were, 1. that Sister Francetta herself was the pig baby, and, 2. that the pig baby was Jesus Christ. There is no logic to either conclusion. Since college I have more or less given up the pig baby. Nevertheless it is a fact that I never look into a carriage without a flush of anxiety. And I cannot get rid of the feeling that Sister Francetta is angry with me.

Apolegit
Joyelle McSweeney

The drunk saint was found with his liver intact which was a miracle straight from heaven. My gumboots caught in the glossies of this fact as I leapt the e-staples. It was below the e-fold, the intoxification unit. My bottles klinked like a cabana full of coca nuts and anorexic soccer goals. My travellin' man thumbed me over to the ravener who approached. When they shared a cigarette through the weeds, I turned tail like a penny.

It made me think of you.

I thumbed and kicked through the flut Seminoles, the fanning delta like two hands kissing at the crook. A dog with extra heads lolled uselessly at the Donut Hole. Give that dog a lemon and he'll fish for a week. The white wading bird rose like a flare or a sneeze, the idiolect Rerun went on snoring at the prow of the punched gut oozing into thicket. When it broke apart he did nothin'.

As for me, I practiced my Jackie Gleason on the shoulder in the spoiling sodium light. My gut arose. I never got home that night or any, I wore the mark of cane like a gold golf club's shaft above the eye. Next noon, I was hitching the road by Oradour-sur-Glane, the town preserved in its ruined, ha-ha, state. I pitched alone, I road along, I was hitched to my own vessel. I probed my garments stitched around me like character development. I bled into my car, I caught the runoff in my nimbly seat. I was like a movie treatment how I held my beginning and end.

How I bargained. My cruet of plot like 'cured alive,' rank as a mount of olives.

It didn't take long. I had as good a grip as the stalks. I made a miracle dress of the dishrag that was a chiffonade in the previous scene. I had ruined the continuity, permanently, and time stood still in shock.

I reached through to the key in the lock which knew my secret like a wise child. Like an old fragile glass that could hold only ghosts shot from the empty stomach out: the kitchen was a moon resort. Every surface grey with food substitute. I climbed into the chiffarobe and made like a stack of plates. I made like a dusty dress, like an illusion. I read a stack of waiting plays, thumbed my way through the roles.

When my tramp arrived I jumped the apple cart, a professional dusty rose. I was an ingénue again. I folded frilled and strategically in and out of the doorjamb. Was I bigger than a breadbox? And the answer was always no.

The answer depended. Was it always or was it repeatedly. Goodbye, dusty rose! Our popularity lagged when our disasters got too polished, the house fell beautiful as a blossom folding open, the ship sunk like a pen in the breast. I couldn't gain money. The types were bankrupt, as were the banks, going under, collapsing with all hands. It was the séance craze, but the bad news glutted space and made the telepaths grit their eyeteeth.

I went over and under bounds to my post-dated embryo lolling outside the pitch and hour of regulation play it had been posted post restante. Do you mean a parcel inside me or the tissue I was digested over and over again? In the green box like a cricket pitch slightly sick from travel, slick from wear. Drop a quarter in the slot and see the green lady going seasick above the tilting benches. That's your mama. Dripsomania they call it when you take your sealegs to land.

I paid for it, signed for it with an equal sign, in that mice writing you picked up in the lycee along with that accent like a case of lice. I hate how your words run mealywormed out of your lips around your cigarette like rats from a burning ship: smoking and bitching.

Dear Kid: I can bitch you out of any state in the union; today it's Kansas and France. I've scraped my hair straight back to the skull in stripes and mounted the bike with my feet shoved into the regulation feet. In this scene, I'm aggressive as a canker, something white and stunning the roses in display. They spot like rain in the black and white picture.

Which is more vulnerable: a glass held up to Nature or Nature depressed to black and white with the night all around us like a showercurtain salesroom. In this scene, I grasp the whisk-broom and lift away to stir the clouds up to an incomparable engine. This magic lacks delicacy, unlike that father-and-son team laboring for life on a collection of smashable flowers. It was no sacrifice to display me in my first role as Baby Moses. Cough-syruped, I smirked away. I strummed my ukulele. In my ancien regime, I sang to the stars while they escaped from the clinic following the leaky bucket in the sky.

Typically, I arrived. Untypically, I held back. What jerk would be there with the stovepipe trousers with the piping like: walk the line. He kept threatening to come pound me when the ground thawed but I'd made friends with the haulers all along the line. When the cruiser docked at Kansas, I stepped down from the stainless steel deck with just a quick look back over my fox stole.

With the toe of my T-strap, I flipped up the backdrop and diverted. I found my self back on the old dry road: Shoebutton! I mourned like a wolf. I tied an old rag to my jaw, reverted, foot stuffed backwards into the kiddie shoe that pinched. Dustamyshoe. Squint-eyes. Drug my chifforobe up the cornfield.

We Make Mud
Peter Markus

Look there at our father. Our father, see over there, he is digging, with his shovel, down into mud. He is, with this mud-crusted shovel, lifting the mud from over there where he is standing, hunched over, and he, our father, he is dumping the mud out, into a hump-mudded pile, here in this other not so muddy place, up here on this hill that is up hill from where the river is, up here where there is this grass up here that is trying to cover up the dirt that us brothers and now our father too—we like to take dirt and make dirt turn to mud. When us brothers ask our father, what is he doing, what our father says to this is, he says, he is working. Working? we say, we say so with our eyes. Work, no, work, work was back when our father used to have a work to go to, back when the black-metaled mill that now sits there on the river's shore, so dark and silent, back when it wasn't so dark and silent, back when blast-furnace fire and smoking smokestack smoke used to make us brothers raise our eyes up to look up at the sky. But now that place where our father used to work, it is a shipwrecked ship with no treasures left inside it. Sons, our father says this to us. I'm making mud, he says. I'm taking mud, he tells us, and I'm making, with this mud, I'm making, out of mud, a house for us to call our own. A mud house, our father calls it. A mud house where mud, it'll be okay for us to walk inside this house with mud caked on our boots. That sounds like a good place to us, us brothers, we say this to our father. And so, us brothers, being the good boys that we are, we drop down onto our hands and knees, down in the mud, and we get to working. We start at the bottom and make our way up. But a house, a house made out of mud, a mud house: this we do not make. Us brothers, what we make, from the mud, we make Girl. We make Girl's knees especially muddy. Girl's knees, they make us want to stay forever kneeling. It's when Girl stands up from the mud that's sticking to the skins of our muddy boy hands, it's then that we can see that Girl, she is naked. Brother is the brother of us brothers who is making Girl's nakedness seem like not such a good thing for Girl to be. So what if she's naked? That's what I've got to say to this. We're all naked underneath our clothes. But maybe, Brother says, maybe she's cold. Maybe she wants some clothes. Are you cold? I go and ask Girl. Would you like some clothes to put on top of your girl body? Girl doesn't say yes or no to this. She just stands there being naked. Brother turns though and runs away and when he comes back he has in his arms an armful of girl clothes. Where did you get those? I say this to Brother. Our mother's closet is what Brother says to this. I give Brother this look. There is this look that us brothers, we have this look between us brothers. It's the kind of a look that actually hurts the eyes of the brother who is doing the looking. Imagine that look. Where else was I supposed to look? Brother says. I don't know where or what to say to this, and so I don't say anything. I take back looking that look. Then I take hold of Brother's hand. I take out of Brother's hands this dress—it's a dress with yellow flowers on it: a dress that I cannot picture our mother ever wearing this dress—and then we slip, we tug, we struggle, we pull, we fight, we rip, this dress down over the top of Girl's head. But even so, Girl is still beautiful. Girl's beauty—it shines— the beauty of mud, it is shining, from beneath our mother's flowery clothes.

The Source of Authority
Diane Williams

A sad story I heard is that I have to have someone take care of all of the bothersome aspects of my life. Tooth, leg, wrist, vein.

It feels so unsexual to complain, but when the weather is bad I go walking. I wander about, but I go to the lake because I believe the lake is better than I am and I want to be in good company. Its beauty, its success, its remote aspect, its inability to speak, hints at intelligence and virtue more pure than mine, better.

The lake means something. I rub the lake and my veins wriggle. I try to make a few things real.

There is so much silver.

Occasionally the lake looks at me coldly which gives me the creeps.

I have had no subsequent conversations with it. We speak about nothing, I tell myself.

On the shore, to myself I say, "Do you really need all of this? It's so crowded. Do you really need all this?"

I am trying to be independent. Is that wrong?

Das Lied Einer Mutter
George Looney

Mozart hears the wind in a bottle of cheap burgundy at four in the morning, awake beside his favorite whore sleeping in the hallway fountain of some Count whose name Mozart has forgotten. Mozart, dry, lies on the carved stone that contains the warm water her body is partly immersed in, the color of her flesh barely altered by her clinging undergarments. Last evening, he performed a new violin concerto for the first time and everyone loved him. Now, the wind in the burgundy is a whisper. *Father again*, Mozart thinks. But this time it's different. The whisper isn't words. At first Mozart thinks it's one of the peacocks the Count lets roam the house. Then he knows it's a melody. Mozart puts his hand on the neck of the woman asleep beside him. A peacock walks by, silent. Mozart closes his eyes and the wind across the lip of the empty bottle, in the time counted out by the calm pulse of the woman, becomes music inside him. When he has it, whole and perfect, Mozart feels his mother smile, and knows he'll never play it for anyone.

He stepped out of nowhere. You hadn't seen him walking, hadn't seen him at all, but suddenly he was there, running across the road. You hit the brakes hard. You've hit him, you think, see his body bumping up onto your hood, his face shattering the windshield— your secret terror: to kill someone while driving. But the windshield does not shatter. You've only bumped him.

You roll down the window to yell at him or apologize--you don't know which—you're frustrated and flabbergasted, "What the hell do you think you're doing?"

"Could you give me a lift to Bainbridge?" he says in his scruffy British accent. He wants a ride. It's his technique, you realize, for getting one. Stopping a car in midstream— and because he's caught you off guard, "Go ahead, get in."

You can't say anything, still shaking some—you almost killed him—how about it then? Was it your fault? And know it wasn't, but know also that if he'd died, you'd have lived with the guilt for years—regardless. But he interrupts. You hadn't wanted to be reminded: someone else is in the car with you. You like your solitude and besides you know your car smells: sour milk from spilled coffee, perspiration mixed with something like soy sauce—it's your private space and whatever made you let someone in? But you almost killed him. That's enough, isn't it, to shake off habit, that covering you always wear—that's enough, isn't it?

"You aren't from here, are you?" he says.

You avoid answering him, counter with a question, "What about you?" but realize it sounds like tacit consent, no I'm not, what about you? Well it's none of his business—why should you tell him that you summer here and have for years? You owe him nothing since his life was spared.

But he's still sitting there, expectant. You realize he hasn't answered your question. Did you even ask it? You begin to wonder.

"Mind if I smoke?"

"Go ahead," you say for the second time, wonder what's made you so compliant, realize it must be his accent, scruffy British and charming.

When he offers you one of his hand-rolled cigarettes you take one, start to believe it must have been fated, your bumping into this stranger from out of nowhere and that sort of thinking, "magical thinking," a shrink would tell you, is only the second of many mistakes you'll make that evening.

Hinges

Anthony opened the saxophone case, put the thin reed to his lips and blue a honking sound like a goose shot out of the sky. He heard his father tumble down the stairs and blue another sound—the walls cracked open and there was his neighbor Mr. Palooka in the clearing dust, leaning in the white claw-foot tub, cigar chomped between his lips, the Tribune quivering between his hands. Anthony blue another great noise and the roof blue off, leaving nothing but the sky far above him filled with great clouds round as whole notes. Anthony ran his fingers over the gold keys, his sound breathed his bedroom door open, carried around the corner to eavesdrop on his sister talking on the hall phone, his mother bubbling up a pot of spaghetti sauce, his sound entered the sauce—a minor chord, *it's too spicy* his mother said out-loud, looking at the wooden spoon, *how did I do that*—he blue another note, blatant and brash, it brushed a tanker-truck on the highway, the driver turned, swerved, saw no one coming—Anthony danced his fingers over the keys and gasped and blue a furious flurry—slap the high hat, heard Ms. Donatowski shouting *smack my ass.* Anthony blue the walls of the apartment tumbling, leaving bare butted Ms. Antonini, Alfredo-the-Kook, Clarence-the-Glue-Sniffer, the Widow Donatelli sleeping with her arms on the chair, drunk and half-lidded, Anthony blue her a new beehive hairdo, erased her wrinkles with wind, hiccup of an old Babushka on the El, blue the bus backwards, the blues blue and his fingers flew like birds, honking and razzing and squeaking like mice as the traps snap, balsa wood broken bones, mine shafted deep wailing, Anthony tongued the reed, thought sound round as a Ferris Wheel, oval as a nun's face, sound like snow hushing against the bars of a prison cell, pristine prism, deep driven as Death pushing the Peddle on the south side of Chicago, blues aging hymn flicked, fifth-flatted his pork-pie hat—worn on a slant— pin stripes and pool halls, bar smoke and husky voiced women—Polly the waitress pausing in mid-riff to say, *that man done blown Cherry blossoms across my lap.* Anthony blue his neighborhood, factory work and his father's lost third finger. Angel the whore licking strawberry jam off a spoon, blue alimony payments, blue electric bills and fancy pants Pauly, transvestite Tommy Depola dancing on a stool in the Civic boiler-room for the Irish City Counselor, blue years off his brother Jacob's parole, blue Ash Wednesday and Easter dinner, he blue Vigilia, welding-torches, jack-hammer-drills, blue Hank Sepeski stabbed three times in the chest outside the school auditorium, cutting class to smoke a joint, blue Tony D.—best cartoonist in his eighth grade—head bashed in with a tire jack because he was Black on the wrong block—wrong time tocked, turned clocks inside back, he blue train rides toward whatever-you-got-in-your-pocket, that cost twisted, short ribs and rice, he ticked the notes into shape shifts, blue the laundromat at 2:00 A.M. watching the dryer spin, eating Ho Hos with nothing else to do but chink two quarters, five dimes—Anthony heard his father home from the plant, heard him swinging his mother like a lunch pail through the kitchen and laughing, calling *Anthony*, who opened the saxophone case on the bed as his father stood above him—*got it off Max the bookie for a case of beer, some chump left it in Douly's bar, dumb Dago—you're going to be the next Stan Getz, go head.* His father snapped on the neck joint, fit the chipped reed, held it said *this is how you grind your axe, I played in high school, haven't touched one a these in twenty years.* Anthony lifted the reed to his mouth and—spit—not a sound except spit, he rearranged lip, sucked in and blue— bebop till the night he sprang up pale faced and powered for one last riff— blew the casket lid right off its hinges—

Lyric Poetry After Auschwitz, or: "Get the Hood Back On"
Kent Johnson

"…[T]he guard force should be actively engaged in setting the conditions for successful exploitation of the internees… by MI (Military Intelligence)." –Maj. General Geoffrey Miller, Commanding officer of U.S. detention centers in Iraq, in internal policy recommendation report, August, 2003.

What's up, Ramal, I'm an American boy, a father, two children, graduate of Whitman High, where I was a member of the Science Club and Student Council, then I got to be the youngest elected officer ever in the history of my town's Rotary Chapter, I'm in charge of fund-raising, which hasn't been easy the past few years, what with the economy and all, but we're hanging in there. I hope you won't take this the wrong way, because I don't want to assault your sensibilities, or anything like that, but I want to be up front with you because I believe that honesty is the best policy: So, I'm going to put a pointed plastic hood on your black and blue head, and then I'm going to stand your caped body on a milk box, with live wires taped to your outstretched hands, and then I'm going to count to ten, you witch-like Arab freak, and maybe I'll flip the switch and maybe not, it all kind of depends. By the time you get to MI, you'll be softened up, and you'll tell us where the terrorists are.

Hi there, Hazaj, I'm an American girl, former Vice-President of the Heartland High Young Democrats and Captain of our Regional Championship pom-pom squad, which no one ever expected to even make it to the second round, it was just amazing, we had our pictures in all the papers and stuff, you should see my scrap book. I hope this isn't awkward and uncomfortable for you, and I hope you don't mind my starting out by just getting straight to the point and saying so: But I'm going to fuck you in the ass now with a fluorescent light tube, you sorry-assed, primitive thug. By the time you get to MI, you'll be softened up, and you'll tell us where all the hidden weapons of mass destruction are.

Welcome, Kamil, I'm an American girl, nineteen, pregnant, my Dad is an alcoholic, but my Mother is in recovery, with her own Daycare, and I'll be taking it over after the Army, I've always wanted to have my own business, and I'm going to expand beyond just one location, I'm not thinking small. And since I believe it is always important to say what one means and not beat around the bush, I want you to know something: I'm going to hold a pistol to your head and tell you to jack-off, while you recite the Koran as fast as you can, you heathen, Hell-bound fuck, and then I'm going to look at the camera with a cigarette dangling from my sultry, teenage lips, giving the thumbs up. By the time you get to MI, you'll be softened up, and you'll tell us where the missing evil Baathists are.

A pleasure to meet you, Khafif, I'm an American boy, former Homecoming King and now Little League coach and Assistant Manager in-training at Wal-Mart, which is providing jobs and low prices for our depressed area, which has been really hard hit ever since Maytag left town, life is tough sometimes. I hope you won't mind my directness, but I strongly believe men should say what they mean, without pulling any punches, so here's the deal: I'm going to shove a fifteen inch dildo down your mouth, while you crawl all over your naked comrades and they crawl all over you, as if you were all a pile of maggots crawling on the rotting body of a dead Imam—don't whimper, motherfucker, or I'll shove the rest of it in, you towel-headed, perverted piece of filth. By the time you get to MI, you'll be softened up, and you'll tell us where the gangster friends of Saddam's demonic sons are.

Nice to meet you, Tawil, I'm a single girl, with an on-line degree in Social Work, a member of the 700 Club and my church choir, and I'm completely against evolution, which goes against the Holy Bible, as you may or may not know, but in the new Iraq you'll get a better chance to know it for sure, and maybe you'll be saved. And because I believe people should always tell the truth to each other, no matter what their race or creed, I'm going to give it to you straight: I'm going to make you suck the cock of your comrade Wafir, until he comes in your mouth and you swallow it, unless you want to get packed in ice like all the other ones at all the other detention centers besides this one, and then I'm going to put a leather collar around your neck, because it's come down the chain of command, a long, long ways, and then I'm going to clip a leather leash onto it, and then I'm going to make you follow me down the long hallway of Abu-Ghraib, squirming like a slug, crying out in falsetto the names of your tent-wearing wife and your babbling, lice-ridden sons. By the time you get to MI, you'll be softened up, and you'll tell us where all the videos and photos of Saddam's torture prisons are… We know they are somewhere, hidden in some deep, wet place, you Babylonian, porn-loving fag. And we're going to get what we want and what we need, no matter how deep down we have to dig. Look at the camera when I talk to you, asshole, or I'll go get the dog.

Hi there, Madid, I'm an American poet, twentyish, early to mid-thirtyish, fortyish to seventyish, I've had poems on the Poets Against the War website, and in American Poetry Review and Chain, among other magazines, and I have a blog, and I really dig Arab music, and I read Adorno and Spivak, and I'm really progressive, I voted for Clinton and Gore, even though I know they bombed you a lot, too, sorry about that, and I know I live quite nicely off the fruits of a dying imperium, which include anti-war poetry readings at the Lincoln Center and the Poetry Project, with appetizers and wine and New World Music and lots of pot. And because nothing is simple in this world, and because no one gets out unscathed, I'm going to just be completely candid with you: I'm going to box your ears with two big books of poems, one of them experimental and the other more plain speech-like, both of them hardbound and by leading academic presses, and I'm going to do it until your brain swells to the size of a basketball and you die like the fucking lion for real. You'll never make it to MI because that's the breaks; poetry is hard, and people go up in flames for lack of it everyday. By the time any investigation gets to you, your grandchildren will have been dead over one thousand years, and poetry will be inhabiting regions you can't even begin to imagine. Well, we did our best; sorry we couldn't have done better... I want you to take this self-righteous poem, soak it in this bedpan of crude oil, and shove it down your pleading, screaming throat.

Now, get the hood back on.

The Neighbor's Dog
Jamey Dunham

The streets are no place for little dogs. The rain beating down on the discarded couch, the leather breathing hard. The small eyes of cigarettes blinking in the alley. Tomorrow the junkies will suffer a great defeat, tonight they coo like kept pigeons. A child is a dog if you look hard enough. A dog with a matchbook of fireflies, playing in a field. A dog running with scissors through the pages of its parents' wedding album. I'd like to drape the neighbor's dog in my arms, stand at the crosswalk and wait for the clouds to part. I'd tiptoe gingerly down the glass-laden streets, careful not to pause too long at the butcher's window. I'd make sure to pass chalk outlines at the feat; fully aware gravity is an absurd landlord. We'd pop into the soda shop for an eggcream, some button-candy and we'd be gone, leaving only the sewer grates to gape in wonder at our passing. The streets are no place for little dogs. Much reeling in of fishhooks from darkened lampposts. Much multiplying of mailboxes when you aren't looking. Beneath every manhole cover sits a man, crouching like a spider. In the air above your forehead, your breath twists like a doll on a shoestring. The streets are no place for little dogs. I place it in the seat beside me and slowly drive away.

Leaving Places
Anthony Tognazzini

There was a guy who wanted to leave, always saying so, always telling us, "This is it, I'm really leaving." We said: "Go ahead and do it." "Nothing here is interesting anymore," he told us. We said, "Go."

So he packed his khaki pants, his checkered work shirts and his *Collected Works of D.H. Lawrence* and bought a bus ticket to Santa Barbara where his cousin worked in a coffee shop and promised to give him a job: Serving scones, cleaning the coffee grinder.

Two months later, the guy came back. "I never should have left," he said about the place he'd returned to. "Why'd you let me leave?"

The place he'd left and we still were hadn't changed in those two months, or it had changed in such imperceptible ways that you would have needed a magnifying glass to notice.

The more romantically minded among us were curious. "Did you charm the hearts of any young ladies?" we asked. "Oh yeah," the guy said, "I got married." *"Really?"* we said, and made him sit down so he could tell us all about it. "Not much to tell," said the guy. "She was a customer at the coffee shop and when I served her double-latte I said, 'Don't burn your tongue.' After that she kept looking at me over her copy of *Dianetics* and blinking her eyes." "What color eyes?" we asked and he told us the green of traffic signals.

"Then," he said, "we went on a date to see a Russian play in which the terrible step-father is a drunkard and breaks all the furniture in the house. Then we went to her place and kissed and three days later over a breakfast of omelets I popped the question."

"Any kids?" one of us asked. "I was only there two months, dummy," said the guy who'd left. "Two months is long enough for something to happen," the dummy shot back. "Actually," said the guy, "my wife was pregnant when I left." None of us said anything.

One girl, though, wearing Ben Franklin glasses and a button-up vest—who, incidentally, had also been planning to leave—shouted, "That sounds wonderful, I'm going there." The first guy begged her not to do it, but the girl left anyway. She had a cousin who ran a Xerox shop in Santa Monica who promised to give her a job: Changing the toner, collating paper stacks. We got a post card with a palm tree that read *Having the time of my life.*

Two months later the girl came back. "I never should have left," she said. "Why'd you let me leave?" The first guy who'd left said: "I told you not to go. Are you pregnant?"

To celebrate her return, we took a walk around the town. "Everything looks the same," said the girl. It was true; nothing had changed in her absence, with the exception of a new travel agency and an extravagant, in-blossom rose bush right outside the firehouse. But you only notice these things if you are paying close attention, the kind of attention you give to a place just before you leave.

And we were all, secretly, planning to leave.

Moonflower
Kathleen McGookey

My brother and my husband hated the moonflower vine after the first killing frost, when it wilted, then rotted, on the white wood fence by my parents' front door. *(Did the vine die before or after my father?)* Inside the house, my mother was dying, too, but from the inside, from cancer that spread before we knew it. *(Does it matter what she died from? The circumstances of her death?)* In the hospital, after her operation, she said, *I thought we'd have more time.* Then she told me to check the pockets of her dress clothes for money before I gave them away.

The vine smelled dead—an odd bad vegetable smell, leaves gone wet and translucent overnight. The smell grew worse every day. *(Did it? Or do I only think it did?)* My brother and my husband hated it, but I thought the vine couldn't predict my mother's death. *(Hadn't my baby grabbed a leaf every time I carried him by, and put it in his mouth?)* Nobody had promised the vine anything more than one summer to grow lush under my mother's care, to unfurl its plate-sized blossoms into the night. Nobody had promised it company, either, but a purple morning glory sprouted; the vines tangled together. *(Like sisters? Like a mother and daughter?)* Nobody had promised it would be loved, or that my father would look upon it morning after morning before its blossoms closed. *(How many summer mornings did he look upon it? How many days did it rot before my husband tore it off the fence?)*

Introduction

In our previous report we explored the manual techniques that can be quickly and readily applied to a story, most notably hand-peeling, scraping and niggling, but also planing, griping, sanding, stripping, and so forth.

Yet not all stories will respond to such methods. A story still well-armatured in style might resist hand-peeling as well as many of the other techniques. A single such story can bring the workshop to a halt. Your job as workshop foreman is to identify such stories in advance and process them through a story barker in the first few moments after their appearance so as to regularize them.

Barkers now used in the Iowa fiction workshops operate according to three radically different principles. In one type, style is "barked" by the friction of the words tumbling against one another; in a second type, it is beaten off the story by hammers and flails; and in the third type, it is cut off or peeled free by rotating knives. In all three, style will be more easily removed if it has been given several weeks to harden and dry.

Friction Machines

A practical friction barker is a cylinder 5 feet in diameter and 9 feet long, with a lockable hinged door on one side. A charge of sentences is placed inside and the drum is rotated until the tumbling of the words against themselves and against the inside of the drum removes all trace of style. *The drum should be perfectly smooth inside.* Any protrusion is apt to contuse the story and render it unsuitable for further reading.

Drum barkers are not manufactured commercially, but can be constructed by a small crew from 1/2-inch boiler plate or 6-inch channel iron. Old boilers—cut down, with flues removed, ends reinforced, and holes cut to allow the more elaborate fistules of syntax to tumble out—also make good drums.

One type of mounting centers the axle. The other mounts the drum eccentrically, thus giving to the words a sliding motion that increases efficiency but requires somewhat more power. The drums are rotated at 25 to 35 revolutions per minute by a gear or chain drive. Faster speeds are not required. In operation, the drum is loaded to about 85 percent of capacity. One such charge is about 200 to 300 sentences according to the size of the drum and the stories (blank sheets of paper or photocopies of previously workshopped stories may be used to make up the load if there are not enough pages). Barking takes 12 to 35 minutes for most stories, depending on season, crispness, length of time since drafting, and type of axle mounting.

A two man crew can operate either type of machine, loading and unloading it, sorting the stories, and stripping by hand the small amounts of style which remain. The story should be seasoned immediately before the style manages to re-adhere.

Hammer Barker

Developed primarily for use with longer, looser stories, a large machine which removes style by pounding it off is being used by one operator in the Iowa workshops. The stories are rotated and fed mechanically past a series of small hammers mounted on a rapidly spinning shaft. About 30 h.p. are required to operate this machine. A crew of five to seven can bark from 2,000 to 3,000 sentences per day. Operation must be very skillful if separation of narrative fibers, particularly at the extremes of the stories and around protrusions and irregularities, is to be avoided.

Peeling Machines

Machines which remove style by cutting it off are also used in the Iowa workshops. Two distinct types have been observed. One is essentially a lathe; the other is a small edition of a pole peeling machine in which style is removed by floated cutter heads.

The Lathe-type peeler automatically centers the ends of the story on a power-driven chuck or dog. The story is then mechanically turned slowly against faster-turning cutter heads mounted athwart a motor-driven shaft. A self-contained motor of 17 h.p. is used for power. When turned, these stories are perfectly cylindrical and have no taper. Four men operating this machine can produce from 120 to 200 workshop-ready sentences per hour.

When stories are crooked or have seep, it is necessary either to remove enough sentences to cut out the defect or to hand-clean what the machine misses. This machine removes style from stories of all types and produces cylindrical stories of a diameter somewhat smaller than that of the original. The machine has an advantage in that it creates nearly identical and uniform stories that can be stacked close together and easily mailed in bulk.

The floating-cutting-head-type story peeler, or peeler device, is still in the development stage. It works somewhat like the standard story peeler. Stories up to twenty pages in length are held in position by small dollies running on the rails and made so as to let the stories rotate. The stories are moved forward and rotated by toothed and beveled "bull wheels," the pitch of which can be adjusted to control the rates of turn and feed. A single cutter head, or carver, with 8-inch knives guarded by a metal shield, floats along the contour of the story, removing the style and rough surfaces to a regulated depth and leaving a good clean story with a normal, albeit minimal, taper. The assembly is portable. When actually operating, this machine, with a 5-man crew, will peel two stories per minute. At present this machine does not have enough range to peel both small (less than three pages) and larger stories efficiently.

A Cautionary Note

We cannot conclude this report without a brief personal note on the dangers of story barkers. In our travels through Iowa we saw ample evidence of injuries as a result of incorrect or careless deployment of barkers--thumbs caught in gearage and torn off, lumped forearms from broken and irregularly healed bones, puckered and suppurating scars on irregularly healed gashes, not to mention the thousands and thousands of mutilated and now useless stories. It is perhaps for this reason that many Iowa workshops still rely heavily on hand-peeling or have moved away from the workshop process altogether to require that each author peel his own work in private.

Working with fiction, despite modern advances, still remains a dangerous proposition.

2 10——true boiling point of water at this altitude in this climate in this place in the summer underneath the summer heart and heat, given the mineral residue from the mines and other impurities that have made it into the water, and given the general resistance of the people this far North to drinking water straight without fizz, a lime, or an alcoholic spike. Drink up. You find fish floating gut-up in some of the lakes. Come out and grab them with your hands. Take them home and clean them up; cut out the tumors and they're fine to eat. Though still, in Harriet's opinion, an unacceptable risk. Some things are worth your life and other things are not.

184——temperature of sparks caused by the plowblade on winter pavement after cutting through the epidermis of snow; Harriet always felt it was like the guys who fired off bottle rockets and roman candles on the Fourth while she ate fried fish: greasy, good, both the boys (though just for a while) and definitely the fish. Liz and Harriet would pick up these kinds of boys some summer nights, do their cool-girl smoking thing in the Subway parking lot as the leftover gunpowder haze settled around them like a shawl. Liz and Harriet in that shawl together, boys outside. Harriet more coy, all smolder, no flare; Liz all burn, a bright and flying thing, a beacon.

184——Sparks don't stay at this temperature for long. They're like birds moving swiftly South for winter. Or atoms dying. A flake of dandruff descending to the floor at the end of an aborted date.

114——when she exfoliates her skin by rubbing quickly, this is how hot it gets.

106——as high as her body temperature has ever gotten; scared her father sick what with her mother gone a month before and Harriet bed-ridden and brow hot as a wake-up airplane towel; she made it to the emergency room and they managed to bring it down with ice and medication; temperature she has tattooed on her lower back as her breaking point. The tattoo that she showed to Liz just after having it done at the only tattoo place in town. Liz surprised, for once a step behind—like in a daze. Even briefly jealous, Liz. Temperature of no small excitement.

97——to break the jump between a pleasant summer evening and her breaking point. It rarely gets above this temp. in the Northern end of Michigan, but when it does she has her work to do: the tar and asphalt patches she does on her sections of road (yes she has responsibilities even in the summer that can usually be defined as *lack of snow*, of ice, of good reasons for accidents) are not made for temperatures this high, since studies show it rarely gets this hot and studies show it's cheaper to use cheaper patching materials and have to patch more often than it would be to use the premium patching quick-dry asphalt.

84——Fire danger changes from *high* to *medium*, assuming the humidity remains the same. Memory of Liz glimpsed at night in the parking lot, sharing a beer with Bone Lumberg, that dark spot, that nothingness. (This memory well before Bone and Carrie—a sort of early murder prototype—but without that fit, that spark and blaze.) Memory of Liz this time gone solo.

71——is about as good as it gets up in Michigan on summer nights when Harriet is mostly unemployed, watching *Twin Peaks* or reading, formerly drinking with Liz before the minor snub, the prom, the X the accident, the bleak and blackness after, dreaming of inevitable winter overtime checks and the sparklight of plow blade on concrete or the regular geometry of a graded gravel road.

65——Harriet's grandparents keep the house this temperature in the winter, which is much too cold and requires the wearing of sweaters, insulation by afghan and blanket, and alcohol infusions. Sometimes she wears her snowmobile mittens and full snowplow regalia at dinner to make her point, which entertains but does no good. Harriet promises herself she'll host Christmas next year so she can jack it up.

58——four deaths in Harriet's family occurred at this temperature—summer falls to throat cancer, emphysema, a heart attack, and complications after surgery to remove a lump from the upper arm. Liz said that, given this, this temperature is bad news for H. and anyone H. knows. Liz said God, *Harriet, I think you're dangerous.* Harriet flushed at this declaration, its maybe-irony. She stays away from the phone until the sun has plunged below the lip of the world and the air cools. During these hours, Liz knew not to call, but show up unannounced instead.

57——when the temperature gets this cold or below, she knows—or used to know, until a year ago—she's safe from loss.

55——is unseasonably nice for Michigan between the poles of Halloween and Easter; means either no work for H. or more trouble when the temperature spikes up this high for a day, prompting the melt and rush, unfreezing pipes, because it's always followed by a dive back down and pipes splitting like cooking sausage and the shriek of copper tubing giving way. 55 in summer means a chilly night, no work of course since no snow, which means relief and nights spent reading Chandler, Dashiell Hammett, or James M. Cain, nights embedded in the motions of the plot like a car along a mountain road with snow gusting from behind.

54——after the Spring thaw and the snow has melted from the roads, it's time to take note of the cracks budding in the pavement—those will take some care when the rain stops to cover over. Harriet attends to her road like a surgeon without the sense of crushing responsibility she knows the most human of them must feel. The asphalt patching—not just the clearing of the snow—is her job. Like a naughty, flat black devil baby.

49——the temperature on the bus she used to take to school with Liz listening to crap 80s radio like "I Love a Rainy Night" by whoever the hell sang that, when she used to carve the initials of her and Liz and various boys into the backs of seats to commemorate their love forever. Temperature at which she got her bus privileges revoked and had to get her dad to drive her to school, which meant breakfasts at McDonalds, sausage & egg McMuffins, and the sight of her dad through coffee steam like a winter storm.

46——the roads sometimes steam at this temperature after the rain has passed and the day is starting up; a small pleasure, difficult to share since it vanishes so early.

44——breath will steam in air; Harriet's brother becomes a dragon, goes Godzilla, stomping towns. Gusts of germ-laden breath.

43——she begins to feel like she's on a slide toward winter, no getting off. When she was young Harriet would want to stay in the middle of the slide. She'd hold her feet against the sides and make the rubber scream. She'd cause huge pileups on the playground or when her parents took her to theme parks with the rides and kids with their faces full of spun pink candy.

42——Harriet begins to watch the sky for signs of clouds or precipitation; even when she's out for mediocre Italian food she's glancing furtively at the coats of customers as they come in for evidence of snow (and the ruination of another nice evening out with one of many boys). Sits by the window if she can help it, or at least sits close enough to the door. It feels like in her life she is always by the door.

41——when it hits this temperature, 41-cent coffees from 41 Lumber which is on her road section, though not quality coffee (need it even be said?), nor good conversation. But coffee is an inoculation against the coming cold. Also the number of the highway that begins a half-hour north of her and runs down to the television heat dream that is Miami, a sunlamp in her mind.

40——temp. at which Harriet always thought she would be proposed to, whenever that would happen, it would be outdoors, their breath intermingling in the air before the kiss would bring on a more pleasing and intimate contact; *yes* sounds so lovely at this temperature, and even *I'm just not sure* won't sound like a rebuff, but a temporary hesitation, an invitation for more: even Liz agreed (said *yes* when pressed) when H. told her this. (Liz not meant, she thought, for married life. Liz unbound, like a flashlight beam coming through your finger skin, regardless.) It's still not so cool that the heart can tell, but cold enough to give the impression of colder days to come.

39——how cold it is in the mine in which her father's father worked and died from soot and long days without light.

37.5—at this temperature, the yearly tally of accidents due officially to inclement weather begins. This tally will only grow and grow.

36——how cold it has to be for the mine canaries to die and sometimes cause a panic with the miners running, fearing gas; of course they don't use mine canaries anymore, do they?

35——the road needs salt, so now she's like a nurse, administering a needle to the flat black tarry patient. Would that she would have been a nurse and on the scene when she was necessary. Would that Liz had not gone through the guardrail (and on to what was beyond for her) on Harriet's stretch of road—this coincidence at the least a difficulty in her mind, maybe something unforgivable and worse.

33-30——range of snowball-packing temperatures for Timothy who is still young enough to want to throw the hardest iceball he can find at windows in the neighborhood.

Always gives you sticky snow that won't be snow for too much longer, that might melt down to ground or translate to chilly bruises on a face. Telephone poles losing all the winter ice, that information carried within the lines somehow freer and faster-moving, those voices coded as electrical pulses less encumbered, breathing easier, more honestly.

32——the big one, means death to some, the annual accumulation of the bodies in the morgue then to the mortuary then to the mausoleum—going through the gates of all those Ms on their way to come-spring burial.

32——also tattooed on her back, right below, a spot only four people have ever seen (after the second tattoo), and on which none have failed to remark. Liz of course was one of them, though much later, when she was being stalked and would stay some nights at Harriet's, when she would get those calls and go on those aimless drives with him, listening to New Order, just solo Liz and him (were they friends, what does that mean?), then she would come back to Harriet's to spend the nights. These nights spent drinking themselves into a haze, some nights spent in other ways. Tattoos sometimes freak men out. Tattooed numbers always freak men out. One more good reason to have them, and have them hidden. Control your circumstances. Control your body.

28——temp. at which salted roads used to ice, before they invented the modern kind of chemical salt.

26.6——temperature of the present tense, the second anniversary of Liz through the ice. When you have a thermometer accurate to the tenths of degrees, you can be more serious about the weather.

26——salt time for the road which means going to the monster set of white salt breasts jutting up underneath the bridge with their metal silo bra. It entertains her.

23——temperature at which Liz's breath was memorialized

on glass in Harriet's parents' house during the last-minute pre-prom freeze just before her passing. Temperature at which *Liz + Harriet* was written. Temperature at which Harriet wished she had removed the pane and kept it in her freezer like a trophy bass or hunted winter remnant meat. Like she could have had it taxidermied, mounted on the wall.

21——consider the numbers: at least two hundred in the hospital every winter from catastrophe traffic; an average of thirty die. Add those who lose it to exposure like Harriet's uncle who got drunk and couldn't make it back to the warm recliner and his coffee left on the plate to boil down to caffeinated tar. Add those to the nightly news death ticker, and other ways to go.

20——temperature at which salted roads will ice, no matter what you do.

18——an unexpected September plunge brings her out of the summer reading in her car to troll her section of the highway for danger spots and thoughts of ice. No precipitation spotted for the evening, but she can feel it in her scapula which rings the neck with its tiny pain bell.

14——temperature at which it does no good to scrape or chop the ice away.

5——degrees by which the Houghton National Bank time and temp. sign is always off; it's impossible for Harriet to come to terms with this, considering so much of her life is bound by time and temperature. How much effort would it really take to fix?

3——sex by now is really a chore unless you've got things insulated well.

0——this low means the mayor considers canceling schools, though without heavy winds and blowing snow (meaning low visibility), it's an iffy call. Some people feel a sense of pride in never closing schools.

-9——the plow itself can barely keep warm when it's this cold, so she bought electric socks from K-Mart that don't work worth a quarter of a shit—the single wire snaking through the fabric burns her skin while the rest stays cold and gray as the day. Good concept though an underwhelming execution. Mark those for a return if she could only find the receipt.

-10——in Harriet's opinion, this is shitkicking illegal cold.

-11——tears freeze complete; nosehairs froze twenty degrees ago; so crying will get you nowhere, like her dad's dead dad used to say.

-16——if it stays this cold for long the body will cease its moaning and desist, finally relax into the stiffness and the air and silence, cease steaming, cease all the cogitation, the deeper sense of culpability, of—let's make it tire-bald, slippery as black ice spread across a road—guilt, or maybe of forgiveness, one of the other signs of life.

-19——coldest recent day that she can remember, aside from the windchill factor which the meteorologists say makes it seem so much worse, and which she uses to pad the temperatures to impress her relatives who live downstate. Still doesn't mean it's safe to snowmobile across the canal— look at the temp. pattern of recent weeks to get a better feeling for it, or, better, don't even try it at all. Timothy has a snowmobile and loves to ride across the ice on days like this against Harriet's sisterly suggestion—and he should listen, considering all that's happened. But he's dumb and young. So cold it's like you're invincible, too stiff and wrapped-up to break. Memory of Liz crouched down with that armless boy in the cold, she so kind and he so strange and quiet.

-38——how cold it gets routinely in places like Fargo and smaller towns in North Dakota; unbelievable how they live, though maybe that's where she should go for purgatory, as a step toward becoming invisible in the constant chill, the car-glass crack, and forget Liz and auto accidents and the numbers permanently marked on the body. You have to put cardboard up in the grates of your car to keep the engine block from freezing. Special windshield washer fluid. Extreme antifreeze and oil. Plug your truck into the outlet at night to even have a chance at starting up again come morning.

-40——all time record low in Northern Florida, state featured on the last postcard received from Liz—a running joke between the two of them, the love of stupid postcards: "Wish you were here in Sunny Florida/Georgia/Las Vegas/ Death Valley where the World's Biggest Pecan/Pelican/ Crucifix/Twine Ball is, Yours Forever, Liz." Was this meant as final words? Or was this her intention—to keep up the correspondence even after she had gone?

-44——all-time record low natural temperature in Northern Michigan. All-time record number of people dying that year, but not H. and Liz and not her stalker, all invincible, still young. Memory of the names listed in the paper. Memory of Liz and her near-admiring At least that's one way out and the silence reverberating after. Memory of not understanding and going home alone, being swallowed in the snow.

-268——big jump now, approaching the big atomic, scientific death, this is as close as she knows we have ever come to the big absolute, and this was only in very rigidly controlled conditions—what those are, she doesn't know.

-271——does even light begin to slow, approximating lines then dashes like in the movies? Will her responsibility then begin to fade? She must admit that she's attracted to this clarity, this permanent anesthesia.

-273——which means absolute zero in Kelvin, she remembers, maybe wrong, from school, where she would sit in Chemistry or whatever class it was behind her Liz.

Always facing the neck's back, the fine hairs and salt traces. Harriet usually in pursuit, in clouds of hairspray or exhaust. Maybe it's Celsius, the scale she wishes they'd use—so simple—but it would take some getting used to. Plus there's a certain panache to using the English measures—a way of thinking that is nearly obsolete but that we cling onto with our sad hands and frozen hairs on end.

-273——Everything stops when it gets this cold, even the atoms stop their baby steps and spinning. Even Liz gone ghost and in the paper. Even Liz in action with her crowd of boys who were not all boys anymore. Even Liz with that one boy, her stalker friend who thought he knew that he and Liz were more than friends, that sad and stupid kid, who gave Harriet (after Liz was gone and gone and gone) half a lock of Liz's hair as a memento because (he said) she had loved her too. Even when he had refused to clarify his pronoun ambiguity and left her standing there. Even Liz submerged in the icy water, or buried in the icy ground, even the dead tributaries of Harriet's family, her lonely body, and her brother on his way back from school on his snowmobile, and the atoms within him. Even the sound waves carrying their essential information: messages from Liz suspended somewhere in the air or memory, her last *Don't go, it's early yet*, her last *Turn it up*, her last *I love this song*. This is cold enough to stop the speed of thought, of any kind of life or useful motion. Maybe this is just impossible, so theory-cold. Even her overtime waking daydreams stop when she's worked so many hours she can't see the road in front of her for but keeps it all going out of force of habit and knowledge of her section of road, out of thoughts of Spring, returning, which she knows it will, with its reassuring thaw and the birth of the million bugs. She will spend more time with her road this year and minister to it like a body, heavy, soft. She will treat it like a monument. She knows some guys who piss on theirs like dogs.

This is what I recall about snow inside a very small tiger, about snow in the shape of a very small tiger, about the expansive relics, symbols sewn into silk, the story they told & those who listened, who listening were circled, enclosed in the weave, assuming the miniscule stitch causing the eye of a very small tiger to appear as habitually open, the habits with which one accords a very small tiger the grace of brittle legs & ardent longing & the habitat a very small tiger treks collectively assist those who take full responsibility & those who assail one another gregariously, untigerlike, in translating the outlandish texts, weather stations & amplitude with which one unmaking a very small tiger replaces the paradox of an exact replica with its opposite, both non-very & un-small, lacking striation, emblematic of a suppressed emotion, of the movement a very small tiger makes when protecting its young or padding itself with snow so as to appear larger, or succinctly, a swallowing of the landscape in order to avoid the inverse, the extinction of a very small tiger & those who claim thinking machines inevitably revoke the omniscience one grants the act of taking a very small tiger by the tail, of superfluous yearning for non-flesh-eating mammals & iridescent oil slicks in the shape of a very small tiger, upon which snow falls gratuitously, evoking the experience of physical action as the architecture a very small tiger emanates from, as the ink expended therein & also yarn, lion-envy & the rusting of numerous weathervanes.

The Least Sneaky of Things
Gary Lutz

There were strides being made in human error, and it was middle-school arithmetic five columns wide he had been hired to teach with a couple of stumpy, yellow, mortal chalks, though that was not the half of it. He had been told not to fraternize with the staff, but the women among them would look him over and put a little something forward of themselves—an arm taken up with an enhancive, practiced fidgetry, perhaps—and then give him the full, accumulated thinking behind it. Only one of them will come into much value here. This was a woman with a rutted forehead, and bare forearms gone velummy from the crossings and recrossings, and glasses that did not give you her eyes at anything like their true size. She rucked her face up at him in the entranceway one morning and said, "Have a high opinion of anything?"

The day came, in short order, when he presented her with a splinty segment of a homemade ruler he had fashioned inchily from guitarwood. (He showed her a tonic discomfort to be had by slipping the thing onto the insole of her flat, murky shoe just before the foot itself returned.)

Then a cinder-gray eraser one had to operate wheelwise. (This she appointed, pendant-style, to the intricated linkworks engirdling her neck, all the better to outcompass the strawberry mark hard by the collarbone.)

And one of those all-in-one drawing aids, a thing that was at bottom a protractor, which is to say only that there was a protractor set centrally, pretextedly, into the clear plastic sheet of it, but that was pranked up with off-curving flourishes and cut-out circles the diameter of practically any fattening finger. (To take hold of it almost anywhere, as she was quick to do, was to become a carnivaller for at least the clinched, worldly instant.)

At best, in other words, the man got himself shooed into marriage, married in fact into disease, but it wasn't disease that took her off, it was the sick-abed she fell in with, and what mattered most remainingly was a cushion she prepared for him not long before she left: it was a squarish cushion, big enough to fall asleep atop if you balled yourself up just right, and she had covered the thing anew with blithely striped fabric of a coarse, heavyweight, farewell sort. For weeks afterward, this cushion was the man's lone seat. Then one night a seam came open. A tiny unparting of the threads at first, and then a liplike tear that took on howling length and width as weeks went loudly out. What showed through wasn't the siftings, the stuffings, he would have expected, but an earlier coverature, a dated floral patterning—plushier, staled—that was trouble to touch because of how thoroughly it mongered up the previous, unhelpful life of hers: the off years, the fair shares of misdevotion, the hard water and dirtier looks, the last straws and accelerating changes of heart. It was all there, confidential and contagioned in what he took for rotting cotton.

Only two further things need saying to clamp down even more on it—how the man would have otherwise gone on feeling sure of what was just too much to ask.

The first is simply that there was a pencil he turned his attention to setting out, in secret early-bird provocation, for the other teachers to reach for, then set down again, unstolen, on the deep-pocked countertop of the full-house faculty canteen. It was a worktable pencil he had sharpened to a fetching, irresistible half of its original span, and he had gone and scribblingly reduced the point of it to a long-suffering, well-rounded bluntness, and he had then left it to catch and collect as much as it could of his fellows, because in no time even the least sneaky of things will have already been handled awfully, will have drawn onto themselves a commonwealth of squandered touch: anything eventually sports the lonelihood of people who could no longer keep their hands to themselves. Why then own up to having any further unsanitary use for the people themselves when you already owned so much of what had gone ruiningly through their hands?

The other, final matter is that in the classroom thereafter he no longer had the heart to insist that his pupils "carry" any leftover digits from the rightmost column of workbook numerals to the summit of the column it succeeded. He instead had the pupils laying the surplus numbers aside ("These loose, glutting, ridiculable tidbits of ongoing arithmeticizing" they were now to be called): the pupils were to set them out on the bed of a separate piece of paper, the backmost sheet of the dwindling, unlined tablet, and then he would lead the pupils in tearing the sheets cleanly free, would recite the grave, tribulationary instructions on just how every numberful sheet was to be folded until it was a contrivement just shy of becoming a weak-bodied box, and then each was to be walked single-file up to the desk so that the teacher might give it the completive tuck and fold. His touch was the touch of a precisioner—and the boxes were stacked flimsily tall on his desk as a wall against parents who were overlappingly dissatisfied, who showed up in jumpy patrols of two or three to pull their sons, their troublable daughters, from his classes. The complaints of these parents were onefold and horrible to have been slaved away at long enough to get contained in sound. But looks alone—the roundabout eyes, every wavy mouth keeping the wall of teeth secret—would have told you that the children had been put, at most, only a little further forward on the vanguard of everything going by the board.

Shadowlawn
Mark Tursi

The flowers of evil are bad flowers, but we realize this too late to divert our attentions elsewhere. As a result, we're stuck to the future like a thud. You may wear a red cape and a blue suit, but let me tell you: you're no Donald Duck. Listen to me: this really does feel like a flow chart. We make love like dragonflies—lots of wings. The stormy Mondays collide bare-chested at the podium of who's-keeping-track-of-eternity. The horizon laughter is one big mirage of nothing but space. Behind the pulpit I can sure tell heart-wrenching tales about our poisoned grammar. You should be put down for such thinking. I'm busy as hell, which means burning. I'm on fire with lies about the truth. I'm involved, but she doesn't realize it. Who could tell the doorway to keep open? The sun should have a name, but younger. Small objects wander in and out of my vision, which is full to the brim with things. There's no way to get them out, so we take lots of fun and dangerous drugs to erase our memory of them. This works for the time being, but as we know, time is not an other, so we're back to square one. Ah squares.

Outside they're keeping track of the inside and vice versa. You can make it go with one. We've always known how to keep a stake in things. This way, we're done especially early. Space is big. There's no way to fill it without morals. So we forget about it and just drive. We were in love, and learned to play hotbox using tennis balls and baseball gloves. Soon enough the rains would come, knock out all the dust and we could see clearly again. Our foreknowledge set the past in motion, and we grabbed our things, threw them into one rucksack and carried on regardless of our fear. What's the matter with the way we were before we knew? All this emerging puts smiles on our faces, and except for the beseeching winds our unknown loves stay hidden. Oh how we wish we were from another part of speech! Another inflection? Another tense perhaps? Are those chittering sparrows making discoveries greater than ours? *Here at Shadowland the question is always: O what awful thing are they doing now?*

They turn the dial past one lunatic frequency and onto another. The idiotic proposals are advanced and, interestingly, we accept most of them as truth. But alas, even the dystopias crumble, eventually. How lucky we are to stumble upon lovers licking their wounds like animals after battle. Calling it dark is one way to avoid our evil delights. But, then again, whose to blame if we forget about the time? The alphabet is the same one we've always used, but somehow the corpses seem bigger and more plentiful. If we're going to reorganize, why not keep the irregularities and throw out the rest? We measure our distances through celestial activity and in this way keep our possessions to a maximum. The downslope is tempting even with crosswinds that dismantle the outworkings of our philosophy like clockwork. The perfectability of our leisure escapes us. The stirring tales bring us to a place of more obscurity, which may be why we find ourselves calling the shots with someone else's civilization. But by now, we can begin again: just look, the horizon is draped in red, beckoning.

Prairie Shapes, a Flash Novel
Daryl Scroggins

Of the many trails leading west, one that was seldom used crossed an expanse of prairie surrounded by mountains on all sides. A pass on the eastern rim allowed entry, and another, almost straight across to the west, was the only exit. The grassland of the great bowl bulged and sagged in places, but only gradually. This led to the effect, experienced by drivers of the wagons that occasionally labored through, of an always ambiguous horizon. The sky became more definite than the land, in spite of clouds that sometimes crossed it quickly and sometimes lingered to keep pace with a cart drawn by oxen.

It was easy for people crossing this prairie to believe that they were being judged by silence. It was as if their actions were being viewed, even when night found them under buckboard and blankets, hidden from the gritty light of stars so profuse as to magnify every kind of distance known to humankind. Always there was the sense that either nothing would happen—ever—besides wandering, or that the world would be destroyed in an instant by a comet or some infinite collapse of the ground.

The only structure in the whole prairie was a small house made of clay. Its red walls were the same color as the road beside it, and it lay at the midway point between the passes. The house was built so close to the road that a baby, in his crib by a window facing the trail, could put a hand out and touch the damp flanks of the horses as they passed. Morning-glories bloomed around the window, and the baby's eyes were blue—so those who looked in as they passed often didn't see him there.

His mother made her living replenishing water barrels from a well so deep that the man who dug it was said to have never come back up. The woman generally lowered the bucket only when the baby was sleeping, unless reliable travelers were present to watch after him as she worked.

But one autumn morning the woman awoke with a fever that didn't allow her to escape her dreams. She rose from her bed with the black dress she slept in smoking in the cold air, and she scrawled a note in chalk on a slate. Wracked with chills, her hand shook as she wrote: Please watch the baby, dear traveler—I must find warmth or all will be lost. She propped the slate on a table by the door and fled.

A lone traveler, a man moving on foot in the rarest of directions—west to east—was the first to arrive, and he could not read. The man waited for four days, feeding and comforting the baby—watching for some parent or guardian to return. But one day was the same as the next. Finally, he took up the slate and wiped it clean with a dishcloth. He looked at the blank surface for a long time. He could not write so he drew pictures and symbols he hoped would show that the baby was safe and would be returned. Then he packed what he could find of the baby's things, and wrapping the child in a blanket he resumed his journey.

2.

The woman reached the southern mountain rim with blistered feet and her face chapped by wind. But she did not stop at the imposing wall. She turned abruptly to the right and then about face to the left. Her pacing lengthened with each cycle of turns, as if the dog's habit of circling for a trail had been adopted but flattened into a line. At the end of one cycle, just as she was about to reverse course, she saw the edge of a canyon that led further south. She turned into it and went on. She followed its rocky edge to the point at which the wall across from her drew near and merged with hers in a dead end. With little room to move, her pacing became a kind of davening. And then she began to climb.

She had only scrabbled up a few feet when she found the mouth of a small cave. She looked in, and seeing light she headed toward it straightaway.

It was a tight fit on all sides. The woman pressed forward, tearing her clothes and cutting her hands on sharp stones. Ahead the passage seemed to open upon a larger realm, but the tunnel narrowed so severely at that point that she had to expel all air from her lungs while pushing forward to reach it. For a moment she was stuck and dark spots crossed her field of vision. But she pushed with the last of her strength. She felt her clothes and the skin beneath them shred, but breath came again as she tumbled into a dim chamber.

For many minutes she lay on her back, taking in great draughts of air—feeling it sluice into her blood, cooling her. When she opened her eyes she knew that she had been feverish, and that her fever had broken.

But an odd view presented itself to her. She was on her back and the light she had taken to be a way through the mountain was now above her. The woman sat up and saw the trick that had beguiled her. At her feet lay a glassy pool of water, and above light fell as if through the top of the tallest of chimneys. Light, striking the pool, rebounded to reflect off a wall of quartz. So the way through—or out— was impossibly high, or back the way she had come.

In a panic the woman's thoughts turned to her child, and she wondered how long she had been gone. She saw in her mind the sharp face of a fox that had watched her on her way south. And she saw the child standing in his crib, waiting.

The woman pulled herself back to her point of entry, and only then did she see that the chamber she was in was a geode. Crystals grew in sharp spikes from the walls on all sides, and like the spines in a pitcher plant they lined the edges of the tunnel she had passed through. When she had torn wide grooves in her shoulders without even beginning to fit herself back through the opening, she sat by the pool, rocking. She watched the beam of light arc wide across the wall and finally chase itself out the top of the world. And she knew she would have to become smaller before she could escape.

3.

Dogs barked as the man turned toward the farm's gate, the baby boy sleeping in the pack on his back. He walked up the lane past roses on fence rails, to find his wife waiting on the wide porch. She said nothing, long after he was in hailing distance, and seeing that she made no move toward him the man hung his head.

At last he stood and looked up into her face. Two years away. He wondered when the turning point was, when he had begun to think of nothing but return.

But his wife seemed as tired as he. And he saw then the worn path in the wood of the porch floor, the missing paint, the raised grain of the planks where she had turned, and turned.

She rubbed her hands on her apron, which meant she had already prepared a meal for him. They went in, to table. The boy awoke when the man swung his pack from his shoulders. The man was about to explain when he saw his wife's face as she saw the child. She looked from the child to her husband, and back to the child again, and the man saw in her face more excitement and love than he had ever known her to have. It was as if his failure in the West and the long months she spent tending the farm alone had been erased.

His sleeping wife held the hand of the sleeping boy, and in the dark the man thought of the little clay house in the middle of the prairie. He built stories for himself of the certain death the boy's parents must have met to have left him where cold or the boldest of wolves could have ended all quickly. And he slept then, as a man with a family again.

4.

The woman touched her tongue to water but would not drink. Ten times the light had crossed her retinal room. She passed the time by singing, directing her voice toward the window above her with hopes that her child might hear and be soothed.

She rose, finally, her wounds crusted over, and removed the last of her clothes. She slicked her body with silt from the pool. When she tried the tunnel again her wounds were reopened, but this time her shoulders slid through to a slightly wider space. Only thoughts of her child allowed her to press on against pain, until her hips were free of the edge and she was crawling again toward light.

A full moon showed her the emptiness of the house long before she reached it. She walked faster, panting, and reached for matches as she tumbled through the open door. All empty, and dust on the baby's sheet. She lit a lantern then and saw the slate. At the left side she found a stick figure of a man, with hat and rifle, walking. Then a small drawing of a baby. Then a tall box with a door on it and a dial with numbers—a safe. And finally an arrow, pointing at the safe.

The woman considered the drawings for only a moment before reaching for clothes. She picked up a tin of biscuits and a canteen and struggled to dress herself as she set out—headed west to find the man who, no doubt seeking his fortune as so many did, had left with hers.

5.

The boy grew. His new father showed him the needs of cows and chickens and the subtle weaknesses of fruits and vegetables. And the boy seemed inordinately— wonderfully—avid to learn such things. His mother marveled at the boy's caring ways; but she worried about the way he seemed always to be musing. Often she saw him standing, when his chores were done, in an uncultivated field, swaying with the wind as if he might float away like the milkweed seeds billowing around him. The same look came to his face when his father spoke of his travels west. Always he asked for stories of the open plains and of mountains, and when the tales moved on to cities and forests, the boy seemed to have stayed behind, lingering, waiting.

6.

A city loomed, and the woman made her way through it as if she had set a whole marsh of birds aflight while hoping not to do just that. Everywhere she asked if a man had passed through with a child, but people shied from her, crossing the street to avoid her. A glance in reflecting window glass showed her a gaunt, shambling figure who appeared to have climbed from a grave. She sold the necklace she found around her neck, and found a second hand dress and a place

57

to bathe. She was then able to ask her question everywhere, but still without result.

A week passed, and she was taken to a doctor when she collapsed in the street. The man's face was stern and distracted as he fed her soup.

"What can you do?" he asked.

"What?"

"Abilities. In what way might you make yourself useful?"

Through several spoons of soup the woman thought about how she might answer.

"I can draw water," she said.

"Ah, an artist." The doctor's mouth twitched upward for an instant, then went back to its straight line.

She worked for the doctor, doing the things he showed her how to do: checking bandages, cleaning instruments and floors. She slept in the room behind his office, and when she was not needed she took her question out into the city by the ocean.

A man said—Yes. Said he thought he knew the person she was seeking. He had seen a man and child who appeared suddenly and kept to themselves in a shack near the wharf.

But when she found the place the man was drunk on the dirt floor, propped against a wall, and the child was a girl. The toddler looked up at the woman and raised both arms toward her. And the woman took the child up in her arms. She left a note with the address of the doctor's office written on it, but the drunk man never appeared. When she went back the next day the man was gone.

7.

The boy did well in school. He learned to read and in his practice at the kitchen table he taught his father to read. A rich woman in town started a lending library, and the boy brought home books of poems and books filled with pictures of machines and distant lands. Geography was his favorite subject, and he found places on maps that seemed to him forlorn for lack of roads and towns. He wondered what grew there—what the soil looked like.

The boy's mother smiled when he read poems to her. She told him one day that his voice moved like wind in a field of tall grass, but just then she coughed into her hand and bright blood trickled down her forearm.

He read then of medicine, seeking knowledge as if he hoped to gather years of study in the course of each long evening. In the end, though, when he was almost a man, he came home from the library to find his mother still, on her bed, and his father digging just beyond the garden.

The boy stood by his father for a while, then went back in to cook some supper. When he went back out at dusk his father was below ground and still digging. The man looked up and asked for a lantern. "Don't heat the house," he said, "this could take a while." It was late October and the nights were already cold. The son worked the farm and lowered food to his father, who seldom spoke and ate little.

Then one day he heard a clanging sound coming from the grave. It was noon and his father was illuminated in the hole far below. He had reached a shelf of rock and was banging at it with a maul. The boy marveled at his father's unflagging energy and feared the man's heart would burst before the stone did. But just then the maul gave up its ringing for a dull sound, and on the next strike a section of rock gave way and fell. It dropped through a space of a few feet into a gray blur of rushing water. The father looked down, standing at the edge of the hole, and made no move to catch the ladder as it slid into the water, its whole length going under before it rose again part way, swung flat, and slipped away.

The son lowered a rope and his father climbed it; he reached the surface and was instantly striding toward the barn. There he gathered his tools and pulled out the fine wood he had been saving for furniture he wanted to build for his wife. He built a coffin for her of cherry and bird's-eye maple.

The boy woke when the sound of woodworking stopped. But how long ago had it stopped? He saw that his mother's body was gone and he ran to the grave's edge. Far below his father squatted at the edge of the hole. He was leaning down, holding the prow of the boat-box with his fingers, looking at the woman's face for the last time. He released his hold and the box entered the dark. The boy could not tell, then, if his father slipped or dove, but in an instant the hole was empty but for the hole within that opened upon a river.

8.

The woman still looked for her boy when her work was done, taking the little girl with her. But as the child grew the searching became a habit of strolls and picnics. They went to street markets and brought fruit. They listened to music played in parks and browsed in old shops where all was covered in dust. In one such shop the woman bought a box of watercolors and brushes for the girl. Back home, in their small room, the child took up a brush and began painting as if painting were seeing. It made the woman dizzy to see places unfolding at such a rate. She watched the girl work as if gazing out the window of a moving train. When the last sheet had been torn from the tablet and filled, the woman was seized by a claustrophobia that sent her out into the alley gasping for air.

"I'm sorry, the child said, "so sorry—I won't do that again."

The woman looked at her then with a fierce concentration, and taking her hand she walked in a half-run to a stationers, where she used her week's money to buy paper. She bought a great roll of paper—a roll so large that a clerk from the shop was sent to carry it for her. She gave him lemonade when he had set his load down and he drank two full glasses before putting his hat back on to leave. But as he turned to go he noticed the paintings strewn about one side of the room.

"You an artist?" he asked.

The woman smiled and pointed at the child, who hid her face behind her hands.

"Mercy," the boy said. "She could paint scenes on walls in restaurants and theaters anywhere."

9.

The boy sold the cow and the mules. He sold the hogs and gave the chickens to his closest neighbor, a widow who lived in a house caved in on one side from rot. Then he nailed the barn door shut and boarded up the windows of the house. Of his parents' things he took only a few mementos, and a few items likely to be useful: his father's clasp knife—with its blade almost gone from sharpening—and a pair of trousers and a coat that fit with only a slight scarecrow effect. And he took his mother's necklace.

When he had boarded up the front and back doors, he took a canteen and walked to the grave-well. He lowered the container on a cord until it touched the rushing water and was filled. He drank. The water tasted of stone and metal—and the taste made the boy think of moonlight.

He set out, heading generally west, with the thought that work along the way would suggest a course.

10.

The woman was sick, but she hid it so that even the old doctor she worked for didn't notice. She didn't want the accumulating proceeds of her daughter's painting to be squandered on cures.

She began to watch the world as if from a distance, much as her daughter did when she painted. She came to think that she might watch so quietly from her window as to finally see all she had wanted to see. Streets dropped below her toward the waterfront, and people passed in droves and in trickles. Sometimes they walked alone, their movement a mirror of the motions of crowds. People went in to escape the weather, and came back out when storms passed—like gulls retreating from waves and rushing back again to new washed sand.

Once she saw a boy walking. She knew he couldn't be hers, since hers would be a young man now. But she closed her eyes and imagined herself running down to him, holding him. When she opened her eyes the boy was gone.

The woman rose to set about her work, but sat down again quickly with a pain in her chest. She remembered then how her daughter had once exhausted the little pats of color in her paint box, and had painted on with only water. Blue and gray images unfolded, as if scenes from a land of summer were set in snow.

11.

The land the girl painted lay to the east, wistful patrons said. She had begun to lose commissioned work on murals because of a new sadness that had entered her work. A blankness of sky and landscape in her painting rose through even the most precise and artful details. Her employers couldn't say exactly what was different in her efforts—only that it now left them wondering about all they would never live long enough to see.

The girl was not disturbed by these developments; there was little reason to continue her paid work since she had discovered the money her mother saved for her. She wondered how they had managed to live with so much of what they earned being set aside. And she found the notebook in which her mother, already sick, had put down brief glimpses of her days in a small house in the middle of a plain. The girl read and heard in her mother's words the sound of wind in grass. Words combed out in a rhythm as soothing to her as the memory of being rocked in a rocking chair.

She headed east, believing that an ocean would stop her, wherever it might appear.

12.

The boy followed a map his father had made for him in the blank end pages of a children's book, and along the way he read the book again—tales of children adventuring in a wild land, protected by abundant luck and hints of a capricious providence. Rain sent him into an uninhabited hunter's cabin, and he settled into the quiet of it so fully as to wish for nothing else. Days passed with little done outside but the gathering of sticks.

Then a hunter appeared, dragging a pile of meat on an elk hide. The boy went out and helped him with it as if an agreed division of labor had long been in place.

"Nice fire you have going there in my grate," the hunter said. The boy nodded, warming his hands by the fire as the hunter did.

They cooked elk steaks, watched the drip of grease. And when they had eaten the hunter produced a bottle of rye and filled cups made of wood and horn. The boy took a sip, but was more interested in the cup than its contents. It was more like a bowl, really; the wooden base was like a stump, with its roots cut to form a level standing base. And the wood at the upper edges where the horn vessel was enclosed was minutely carved into a mountain range.

"I don't just hunt," the man said. "Come to town with me tomorrow."

The man opened a sliding warehouse door to the smell of sawdust. He lit lanterns and showed the boy his wood working equipment.

"Mostly I make bowls," he said. "But there are other things."

The boy looked at walking canes and carved pistol grips—and a tiny village in an eggshell that could be viewed through a peephole. And bowls. Bowls that seemed to hold and incorporate the hands of those who held them. The boy mused as he touched polished surfaces everywhere, forsaking the world for the maps he found in wood grain. And the hunter knew he had an apprentice.

13.

The girl moved toward the places her painting revealed to her. She had put all that she wanted to keep of what she owned in a handcart, and, dressed in stout shoes and a broad hat, she moved from town to town, toward mountains. People streamed past her, headed in the opposite direction; she smiled at this—a refugee headed in the wrong direction.

She walked through mountains. She crossed forests and was ferried across rivers. And finally she came to a pass in a low chain of mountains that curved away from her to the north and south. Some travelers appearing there paused and spoke to her.

"Nothing ahead but a big prairie and a pass at

the other side," a woman said. "No place to stop but an abandoned house in the middle, but there's a good well there. Good water."

The girl went on. Waving grass took hold of the land and the dusty ruts of the one road appeared; she felt herself relax for what seemed like the first time.

She had entered the prairie at daybreak and walked all day without seeing another traveler. When the sun was low in the sky her thoughts turned toward setting up camp. But just then she saw a shape ahead that seemed to stand in the road. It was the small house made of clay, the very one spoken of by the woman at the pass and by her mother long before.

The girl entered the house and straight away sat in a chair at a table, as if she had simply returned from one of many trips to garden or well. The silence around her gave way to crickets; she lit a candle which she found where she thought it should be. And by its light she straightened up the three rooms, dusting chairs and sweeping. She stood for much of the night looking at the baby's crib by the window that was almost in the road. The light of stars fell into it like milk with a blue tinge. She let her fingers trail over the white sheet that still covered the straw-filled mattress, and she followed the lines of dead vines that twined about the bars of the window. Finally she retreated to the bed in the other room, and slept.

14.

The young man set out from his own shop, headed west with a wagon load of bowls he had made. Asian markets had opened on the coast, and they paid handsomely for works they sent on to other lands. He went south first, and then worked his way north along the ocean shore. When all his wares were gone he paused for a day in a teeming city to rest and to eat well before heading east. He went to a restaurant built on a high street that faced the ocean, and as he sat waiting for his food he saw that the walls were painted. They were painted with vistas that seemed to hold no regard for what people usually wanted to see in such views; and when such things appeared, the wanting of them had changed in the course of looking. The man's food was delivered to him but it grew cold as he gazed at the walls all around. Who could have moved a brush like that without being overwhelmed by the world appearing? Surely memory could not hold such a thing, and desire alone could not conjure it. It was the pain of beauty he saw, uncommon but common to many shapes.

The waiter came and apologized for the distraction caused by the "scenery." He waved his hand in a gesture of mock appreciation, and offered to warm the man's food again.

Distracted, the man looked up at the waiter. "If the food was as remarkable as the scenery," he said, "it would not have cooled." Then he smiled, and the waiter, relieved, smiled as well. The man asked him about the artist and heard only that she had moved on. "Which way?" the man asked. "No telling," the waiter said. "Perhaps she's headed back to where she saw all of this," he added, turning to gaze at the images on the wall.

The man paid for his meal and left. And he went on, away from ocean waves. He made his way east, and finally the landscape began to look familiar, though he had no knowledge of having ever been present in it.

15.

The young woman heard the clink of traces and she stepped out into the road in her bare feet. She wore a long dress she had made from cloth acquired in trade; it was pale purple in color and she had sewn rough crystal beads to its hem. She looked eastward for some sign of a traveler, but she was looking the wrong way. Behind her a voice called out, softly. "You were not in the painting I saw, but now you are," the man said. The woman turned to him, already smiling because of the trick of direction, and when she saw him something in her leaped toward him.

"You will want water," she said, shading her eyes.

As she turned to begin drawing it the man called for her to wait. He brought her a cup of wood and horn, with mountains carved at its edges. She held it and gazed at its intricacies, and when she looked up his expression answered that it was what it seemed to be.

She took him in and cooked for him, running out at times to pull an onion from the garden or pinch leaves from herbs. They spoke of their travels into the night. And then they circled about the house, looking for the place each would sleep, and they circled until they returned to each other, smiling, settling down where they were.

They gardened and drew water for the infrequent travelers. The man had brought blanks of fine wood and new tools, and he had on his wagon a roll of paper he used to wrap bowls that were sold. So the woman painted, and wove bags of twisted grass to take the place of the paper she used. And the man carved.

16.

Scratches on a wooden calendar showed the woman's birthday was near, and the man had nothing to give her that was not already hers. She laughed when he asked her what she liked that she didn't have. She told him there was nothing she didn't have. And when he pressed her she laughed and said she wanted knowledge of what the hawk sees. She wanted colors that produced a reliable sound. And she wanted a bowl of shaved ice, dark with the juice of blackberries.

17.

Before sunrise the man packed a lunch of bread and hard cheese, and he drew water for his canteen. He left a note for the sleeping woman that said he would return soon with something she didn't have. And he set out for the north rim of the mountains. He rode the mule, free of its wagon-pulling chore, and in a large saddlebag he carried sawdust. He would use it to pack around the ice he hoped to find, and he would gather berries as he found them.

18.

The woman read the note and frowned, then rocked herself a while. She wished he had not gone. Not on this day, in particular, when she had planned to tell him of the new life on its way.

19.

The man reached the mountains in the early afternoon—
later than he had anticipated. Cliffs rose above him and he
turned the mule to follow the unrecognizable circle. When
he had gone at least two miles he despaired of his task and
pulled up, resolved to turn back for home. But just then he
saw a white wall between mountain teeth. Ages of snow
had slipped to a shaded cleft in the rock, and like a glacier it
rode the inverted triangle and calved to melt water where it
met the sun. So astonishing was the frozen structure before
him, the man was not content to gather cold shards and
pack them away. He tethered the mule loosely to a hank of
grass and climbed the rock beside the ice.

At the top he paused, and he marveled to find the ice
stretching like a road before him, a road headed north. He
walked the rough surface and his shoes crunched with each
step. He walked as if on a great pier that extended out into
the tops of trees. He slowed when the ice began to slope
downward and decided to turn back. But he slipped. He
laughed at his clumsiness, and dug in with the edges of his
shoes as best he could. But he slipped further and suddenly
gathered speed. He was tumbling then, with spans of flight
and impact, and then a long fall came in which he called out
his love's name. Tree limbs broke his fall, but not so much
that his leg was not snapped when he stopped in a jumble
of rocks.

When he woke it was dark, and a cold wind was
blowing. The man thought of his love, waiting for his
return. He set himself the task of splinting his leg, keeping
his thoughts apart from his body—as if he were a doctor
tending to an unknown patient. When he could stand and
walk with the aid of a stick, he approached the ice. He
circled its edges, but everywhere its face was glassy and
steep.

He turned then and looked at the land in which he
found himself. It was nothing like the plain. Trees grew
from cracks in rock, and cracked rock showed the work
of present and long dead forests. Walking for a man with
two good legs would have been hard going, but the smooth

incline of ice left no choice. The man tucked his chin and set out, headed for the east pass. The rough terrain seemed to be matched by severity of weather: the temperature dropped as darkness came and gusts of wind made whips of low branches. Morning, though, found the man pressing on—distance and time already gone, already small in the face of a will to be true.

20.

There is a wide plain set in a bowl of mountains. A pass at the eastern boundary and a pass at the west allow travelers to cross, but the trail is seldom used. A single road—two ruts that gently rise and fall—cuts straight across. The only structure in the whole expanse is a house made of clay at the trail's mid point. A woman there makes her living drawing water for travelers. The house is set so close to the road that a baby in his crib, by the window facing the ruts, may reach out, unnoticed, and trail his fingers across the flanks of passing horses.

I am always hoping to deform people into appearance...

-Francis Bacon

I.

If shape is a finished thing, what is this? A black background, a few white verticals, a few horizontals lending depth to a darkness. A convergence of lines suggesting the corners of a transparent box. The tentative outlines of a showcase, or a glass cell, maybe. Or else a room of some kind—the steep tilt of a floor meeting a wall, the wall a low ceiling. Lines that, in their faint drag across the canvas, confine a darkness, & in that darkness the hunkered clump of something human. Bald gore of the un-rinsed under-life. A hunch in a suit or a mouth with a tie. Interrogator? Lover? Pontiff? Something insubstantial. Isolated. A waiting figure blur-bound & boxed-up. Adumbrated but alone. Hardly differentiated from its surrounding space. At no point let to fulfill itself. Everything below the waist open-ended, continuous. Neither elegant nor useful—its sex indistinguishable from a wall. Untouchable. Fleshless. An idea given up on.

II.

Better than memory, better even than love, & more dependable—anger, which ignores the long because &, instead, simplifies, ignores. As Peter in Tangiers. The gin-tinged temper. The brawl. Thirty or so canvases gashed-gone, cast to the cobble below. The abrupt blood on the floor, the rest swallowed. Past gathering, past putting back: an inspiration.

III.

Your imagination—a room. A butcher's stall where the 19th century is taken by surprise. Cleaved with a brush, semblance skinned & splayed. Or hung from a hook &

dangled to drip—the raw haunch of perspective. Because love for you means carcass. Means fresh violence & anything beyond repair. Anything rubbed raw & un-relievable. Flanks sloughed in a bed. Mouths vaguely human, biting at empty air. Stuck open as if to remind us there is no certainty between pleasure & pain. A scumble. A gouge. Meaty shades of red & blue. The absolute afterall: bare flesh & the wound—where the living, the dying is done.

R eading the titles alone is a pleasure. Quinn hasn't got any money in his pocket anyhow.

These types of bookstores are best: used books, dark, old furniture, musty.

The pages of this book—*Lectures in America* by Gertrude Stein—are damp under his fingers, and rough, and yellowing.

They make a soft music when he turns them: the hiss of the coffee machines, or the sound of static when the TV station has gone off the air for the night. Sounds that don't exist any more. Kinds of silence that no longer exist.

What is poetry and if you know what poetry is what is prose…

He becomes distracted by a movement by his side.

Someone else reading the titles. Different than looking for a particular book.

A young man: Tim, the boy who works at the coffee shop.

Suddenly Quinn, who for nearly two years hasn't given a serious thought to being touched, runs his hand through his rudely cut hair.

Wishes he hadn't cut off all the shining curls.

He can hear Tim breathing. Stealing glances sideways.

He feels badly dressed, too skinny, ugly, unprepared.

So he recites Emily Dickinson: *"We don't cry—Tim and I—*

"We are far too grand..."

Tim smiles

but Quinn doesn't know the rest of the poem.

Instead looks right into Tim's eyes and drifts into silence.

(There is no use in telling more than you know no not even if you do not know it...)

They are walking along the rock jetty to the beach.

"So you make sculptures out of trash. And came here to make art."

"Shouldn't have come," says Quinn. "Dumpster diving is better in New York."

Tim doesn't say anything.

Quinn feels like a ghost in an abandoned city.

"So why did you come here then?"

Now Quinn is silent. He looks away across the bay.

Not so far from them, the mainland.

Because of the peculiar quality of light here, he realizes he still cannot discern the place where sky and sea meet.

They pick their way through the dune grasses.

Following the trail.

"At high tide," Tim tells him, "All this is underwater."

Black irises. Deep flowers.

I'm underwater, Quinn thinks.

At the beach, Quinn puts a little distance between himself and Tim.

But watching him out of the corner of his eye.

Tim is young. Like a boy. But acts like a man. Moves physically like a man.

When I was nineteen, thinks Quinn, *I couldn't even look at another man in the eyes, let alone talk to strangers in bookstores.*

He's looking savagely into the storm.

Wanting to be the storm.

Wanting Tim's rain-lashed hands on his skin.

And roughly.

Tim doesn't mind being left behind.

Watches Quinn's little figure up ahead. Black, flickering. A shadow. But of what?

"The wind's getting stronger," he tries to say. But Quinn doesn't hear.

Quinn's thinking:

No driftwood

Rocks — small, polished in the water

The rubble — smashed bones, crab claws, little bodies

He's hoping to see the ghost-skin of a jellyfish spread across the ground.

Doesn't even know if there are jellyfish in this area.

Thinking:

Portuguese Man of War.

The whiteness of Tim's shirt.

The broadness of his shoulders.

He is beautiful.

I am alone.

They walk shoulder to shoulder. Quinn's not sure if he slowed down or if Tim caught up.

They still do not speak.

Still.

Quinn recites a poem he heard once:

"After the storm blew in
Shattered the windows

Cried the doors open
We found the wound, there, deep,
And where it's always been"

Quinn, separated from the only world by acres and acres of water:

"I'm here, not-here, mine, and empty..."

They stay until they can't see the ocean anymore. The sand becomes darker and darker until the grains dissolve into each other.

Quinn thinks, "I'm tired, in trouble."

"What's next?"

Tim's looking at Quinn, thinking, "His eyes when he looks off into space. At nothing."

"Living a past life?"

"His mouth always closes completely when he's not speaking."

The girl wrote a story. "But how much better it would be if you wrote a novel," said her mother. The girl built a doll's house. "But how much better if it were a real house," her mother said. The girl made a small pillow for her father. "But wouldn't a quilt be more practical," said her mother. The girl dug a small hole in the garden. "But how much better if you dug a large hole," said her mother. The girl dug a large hole and went to sleep in it. "But how much better if you slept forever," said her mother.

The Black Cat
Joanna Howard

In unseasonable torrents, the car overturns on the road at the foot of a long curling driveway, the chauffeur's head crushed against the glass. The passengers are unscathed. Thank God, says the American. Of course, now your honeymoon is ruined, says the Hungarian aristocrat. The American looks at the fainting woman in his arms. Well, it's not like that, he tells him, that would be too, too much.

In the hilltop mansion, the bell rings Rachmaninoff. Behind the poster bed's veil, the elemental doctor rises to touch the forehead of his child bride. The hand he passes over her eyes deepens her coma. Stay in bed tomorrow, he tells her, don't tax yourself, darling.

In the foyer, the American blows a low whistle. This place is swank, he tells the Hungarian. It's Deco, the Hungarian corrects, we've got that here, too. The bright high doors pop open with the pressure of a finger on the gilt crossbar, an utter hush. The black cat emerges. The frightened Hungarian shuttles a small dagger at the animal, deftly pinning a front paw to the carpet. Now see here, announces the American.

I, in my crystal box, await the return of my husband from the war.

2.

By then the rain is slowed and stopped. The Mongolian valet cradles the platinum damsel. His mustache is a waxy fake. The path twists up the hill, a mile at a turn. The air holds the storm's cymbal, its precipitous brunt, but the sky lights clear and cloudless.

Soon she will be walking. She can't help the thought of some strange fingers shifting about in her hair as she slept in the railcar, the nails sharply bronzed. In the halls of the great architect, in her effortless gauze drape, she will enter his library like sliding on ice. The bright solid patch of a bandage, discernible under the chandelier's glare, emerges from beneath a frill.

Her eyes are thick, her gestures mute. Do I need more dressing? she asks the writer, perched on the arm of the wing chair. And how, my sweet. Can someone get her an iced tea? he announces to the host. The architect is distracted, already the cogwheels agrind. I'm sure the necessary drugs have been administered, he tells his guest. The effect, as you must know, is always unpredictable.

I'm left with a great deal of questions, the damsel tells her audience, with measured phrasing. Here the black cat begins her third ascent, from death, from the seamless travertine.

Her senses either blotted or more acute.

3.

Behind the Japanese screen, the two great men are alone in silhouette. My trip has been long and arduous, the Hungarian declares.

They say that wars change men, the architect tells him.

That is what they say, but then I have never been one of those kind of soldiers.

I might have guessed as much.

Between these two, some manner of business remains uncovered. They step so lightly on paws, their shadows cross and merge. And what if the question remains unasked: what have you done with Karin?

I am trying to collect some pieces, the Hungarian reminds his host. In my mind, I recall two faces.

One came sooner and one much later.

Had I a daughter?—I'd forgotten. The earlier picture is the one that interests me.

Dead.

And the latter?

Dead as well.

And did they look quite perfectly alike?

That is often the way things go.

I am tempted to thank you for your kindness, Hjalmar, especially if this is all there is to it.

Vetus, we both know that below any great mansion lies a larger, greater mansion.

Often so.

The Hungarian hums low to demonstrate a certain doubt. There must always be something so tangible between things.

4.

In the library, misgiving huddles in the stacks. Again her frills are bristling. The electric candelabra portends a crushing blow from overhead. Her skin glows with crystalline powder.

I slipped out of bed, she tells the gentlemen, cigars smoldering against the trunks of their snifters. Too much satin, she shrugs.

She's a real deuce, the writer announces. Always yucking it up. But while I beg your entire pardon, I can't help wondering, is this the way it should go?

The hush from the ranks is stiffening. They hang on her next phrase, every line farsighted. She lingers angularly adrift. The smile is pleasant at best.

5.

Beyond the peaked windows the dark is firmly settled. No one can guess the hour. The sky awaits a ritual moon. The party, with agitated senses, disperses to the chambers, the staircase a long curling spiral to the third floor.

The Hungarian in his room lays out monogrammed pajamas and a quilted jacket. The writer peels back the accordion divider to light the bed silk. His marcelling is starting to give: one waxy tendril has dropped over his left eye. Backlit, he wears a different age. I can't help but feel safe, he announces. In that case, we ought to switch, the doctor suggests.

For the writer, exhaustion mounts around the eyes. He tucks hands in pockets and offers a rough shrug. I'm starting to feel a bit out of the dynamic, he tells the doctor, who offers a nod of support. Actually he's coming into his own. Seraphic and haggard, like something brought in, he's developed a slight appeal.

The writer twists at the knees. I wasn't cast to play the rake.

No, of course, the Hungarian tells him, but all our parts are shifting.

6.

At the mansion's center, stairs curl up four flights in a perfect cylinder, and the tube that remains unfilled illuminates a spot on the marble from the skylight above. A table has been brought out and dressed for playing. All at once the chess game has begun; the players seated on velvet cushions stretch long legs out from the marble table in a cone's point. The winner will select the sacrifice.

The two young lovers are clad in tweed for travel. The blonde's eyes are smoky and clotted. I don't think I'll ever get a wink in this dump, she tells the writer. It's time to hotfoot it.

Are you vastly improved? the doctor asks her. Her tongue and lips remain thickly numbed. Whose side are you on anyway?

Things are hotting up nicely, the doctor tells his opponent. I haven't played in years, but I can't image I'll lose.

That's the kind of thing I hear a lot, says the architect.

Ciao, the lovers are saying as they slowly step backwards out of the circle. Ciao and thanks heap-loads; they wave at the gentlemen.

In the shadows, the tapestry pattern obscures a hulking figure. The Turkish henchman cracks his knuckles. His arms extend into the light.

7.

Under the house, a fortress ruin is situated, stairwells and corridors curving down into the crust. In the very pit, the séance begins, the gentry stacked thick in lamé sheaths and dinner jackets. The Occultist reads softly from a satanic text, the folds of his kimono gaping black.

The sacrificial alter lines up the chiasmic portrait. The virgin is running late; her hair is being done at a skirted vanity, several floors up, inside the house. I am the very essence of the part, she tells the servant. Look at this

81

bracelet, it really shines indoors. But, you and I know, it's how it looks in the sun that counts.

The Occultist looks thin inside his robes; he seats himself roughly on the edge of the makeshift stage. The audience, impatient for a sacrifice, yawns, sipping from flasks. Once a leader always a leader, the Hungarian tells our host, and takes his hand. Finally, he says, I am of two minds on you.

I'm sorry for that, Vetus. All I want to say is how tiring it all gets.

Yes, the Hungarian admits, that is certainly the case with any profession.

Already the panels of the walls are shifting as the Hungarian strokes those long gray fingers. He hopes for the courage to cut the skin from the bones.

8.

A cellar vault must turn around to align the open doors. So much depends on technology in these ancient systems. The writer may be lucky to break out of his prison, but with each passing hour he puts on character like so many winter clothes. The nature of these stories is that something must give. He is building up a certain charge, and awaiting the release.

This is the level at the very bottom of it all, gouged out of several layers of rock. The mansion above is well insulated; with every room comes a fire glowing out of frame. It might be nice to find the room up there with an inviting corner trap to crumple in. No doubt there are many, but complaints will get you nowhere. The air here is cool enough to keep us looking our best. A fur coat is tempting, but ultimately not advisable. Where will a cat-suit get you these days? Sleep is the key, though my daughter's is periodically broken.

This is the moment when someone should comment on how things hang in the balance. As with a picture, they should not be encouraged to tilt too much. I remain within my glass shelter. In the end, these walls might be razed in strips, like peeling fruit, or they might come down in shards.

Had he, had she the sense of horizon, they would have split like a dried pod and let the periphery blow away. Instead they were conjoined strangers. Two figures, unbeknownst to each other, soldered at the head, bodies angling out like a roof.

One asks the other what they might climb for. The other replies they climb like a ladder, to the height were parallels meld. And then they could go their separate ways. But they are very stable on this horizon, and in this wind.

Between each rung, the world is a different color. Like a lens suspended.These frivolous rungs and their stains. Each color, more afraid of height than the last, deepening. Purest elevation is blue.

They are not joined. Their parts do not touch. The ones most terrified define the sky by floating.

One says to the other: I can see through you. Because climbing is a process so transparent.

The other one imagines falling from the ladder, and she would do it, if she could only do it by herself.

The one says: you have hurt my hip. But the other says: that is not the part that I touched. She says: I won't let go, until you tell me what part I touched. And he imagines her with a wing or a horn, another of the truer appendages.

She is drowsy, each horizon collapsing fuzzily, like a blanket.

She is on solid ground and the collosal ladder balances there, steady, weight equally on breastbone and pubis.

And there it is again, the giant hand, reaching down from the sky to take the ladder, but not from her and the gravity she would supplant.

She has seen them from a distance. Forehead to forehead, perfect in tension. The shape of the world is triangular. Her sight is opposite its sense.That they were a single enormous figure, bent double at the gut, is irrelevant. She wants to be away from weather, and crawls into the cave of limbs.

Rather than a hand, there was a mouth, dangling in air. She admired its symmetry. Its parts met, and split in two, and then blew themselves away.

Rather than anything else, she rose up to qualify what spilled from overhead.

Blowing from Matinicus from Criehaven this wind is a progressive advection, it lacks a consecutive dialectic, is this a hermitage, an unriddling, is it some new trick. Does a bridge cleanse and if so how will the children learn and when, how will they move. And be moved. To move. How will the children move and the wind as it brushes up past Boothbay into Booth Bay and into the river, when or how does a bay become a river or a river a bay, when I step into it, when I or anyone steps, when and what then is a child, did I carry or was I carried or is childhood really this daily island life.

If not why not.

But the wind blows. This is indisputable, this is the nature of wind, one does not have to be a bridge, to build a bridge, to negotiate a causeway to understand, one does not have to pledge one's self to alternative energy sources, it is enough to be a citizen, it is enough to learn. To be a citizen could mean to own a boat. It once meant this.

Low tide at Hodgdon Ledge. Is this a form of voting, have I performed my civic duty.

I have walked to the south pond and back and I have walked Long Cove on the east side and I have walked Long Cove on the west side. I have seen Tarbox Cove and Jewett Cove and Knubble Cove and Brooks Cove and I have walked on the East Shore Road and on the West Shore Road. I walk and have walked and in walking so walking do.

I sing as I walk when I have breath which is not always.

Have I tailored the sea-gale to any prior fallacy, have I discerned: the germ. The pattern. The sortilege, the apocalypse, the subliminal response.

To the traditional hexachords (hard/natural/soft) Guido d'Arezzo added the device known as the Guidonian Hand. Eleventh century. A physical mnemonic, as shin for sound or thumb for shoal. Gastrocnemius, the belly of the leg. *Ut re mi* now modernized in the movable-doh which some use which some do very well use but not so different not so very different no.

Oil sheen. If one makes a fetish of furniture can one travel there.

I score these words with my fingertips. Over the bay a lone tern is wheeling. There is not so much, not so much as I had thought, not much though it is enough, I thought, though I think, though I say, though I will never say it cannot be enough, I was once a child, it is enough to have been a child and to have known this, to know and to be, to ferry, to cross, to apprehend is to remember and it is enough, I know. I am. And so the music makes me.

I know I've read the beginning before, maybe last summer. I picked up the book and read some few pages. Now however that I'm about a third into it the story still seems familiar to me and I'm wondering if indeed I read exactly this far, as far as I read today, or if the unfolding of the story was so obvious that even though I didn't actually get this far before, I could predict that I would recognize the new characters who've been introduced and that I would be as uninterested in continuing to read as I was last summer.

Of course this makes one think about why one wants to read in so beautiful a spot anyhow where there are any number of other things to do: swim, walk, stare at birds. Today I tried staring at the birds, but after a while, no matter that I was also sunning myself, doing two things at once that is, not just one, I found myself wanting to read. The birds were interesting and even predatory, but I couldn't get into it. So I reread the article in the newspaper about the guinea hens which people are keeping on their lawns to eat the ticks that cause lime disease and which people are very glad to have even though the birds make a sound like fingernails on a blackboard and even though their lawns are now full of holes where the guineas have gone after ticks. They are good at it and some feel, so the article says, finally safe though they check their children all after just to make perfectly sure. The whole thing seems rather tedious and the article was endless so I didn't finish it and when I looked up the birds had gone.

So I return to the novel I might have read before and am especially attracted to the dampness of it, the boys lying about in damp bedclothes, the dampness of the city on canals, and the damp eroticism of the novel because it so matches my own situation here in the cabin in which I am damper than ever before and also the towels and dishcloths and the floor even seems damp under my bare feet because it is summer and I am always walking in bare feet in summer, often with a book under my arm. And the pages of the book turn and curl in the downpours and residual damp. The sound you hear in the background actually is not the birds which I was listening to before, but the drip off the leaves in the woods where the cabin is located. The dog drools on guests who come by although there have only been two in the last four years so you'd probably not notice this particular feature of the place. I watch the covers of the paperbacks curl. It is so noticeable that one cannot help, unlike with the drool, noticing the curl which usually occurs out of one's sight, at night or when you have left the room and return to find the cover curled, unless you remember to weight it down with other books, preferably hardback books which the current novel is not nor is it hardcore, though as I said, decidedly damp and erotic and so plotless as to seem familiar, as if one read about the boat ride in the canals previously, although now I am sure that last summer I didn't get this far and that the covers were more or less flat.

And of course I feel guilty because I ought to be doing something other than reading and I ought to lift weights, but I can't seem to stop reading except of course when I stop reading to do something equally useless like throw out bread crumbs for the birds and see what comes or fall asleep and into such a deep sleep I am with the boys in the novel throwing off bedclothes in the damp heart and throwing my legs about and scratching the scabs I have gotten from insect bites because of the holes in the screens. At night the moths come in and distract me from reading and sleeping which are the only things I do well except I have begun a list of the different sorts of moths even the ones which have died by morning and look like dried up brown leaves. So far my favorite is the copperglaze moth, metallic and quite small, about the size of a thumbnail, and it also has the advantage of not flying about much so that in the midst of an unread paragraph one can look steadily and not have it bang into the light which one must have on if one is to get any reading done.

So I return to the book I remember so vividly and yet vaguely and a central narrator with whom I cannot identify in his essentially plotless story and find myself thinking how much his experiences and mine are alike as he tries to pursue his tasks in the midst of increasing dread. It is the dread that does it, the summer dread that is absolutely the worst since it's based on so little information about the sorts of ticks and spiders and moths which surround one and are so simultaneously invisible as one is going blithely about one's business of reading the books one has to read in the course of a summer vacation.

What the main character seems to dread is some dissolution into the books he is reading which he feels are encroaching on what used to be his firm sense of identity; he was writing something or doing research on something, but in the midst of all this quiet ordinary endeavor he finds himself feeling a sense of dread from the dangers of the city in which he lives and from an array of unusual circumstances which seem not exactly unusual in any bizarre or outlandish sort of way but just slightly unexpected. And of course I can't really identify with this urban dread since I'm in the woods and have no fear of helicopters flying overhead and shining searchlights into my window, but nonetheless as I read further in the book, I find myself unable to lie about dazedly as I was wont to do. Rather I find myself unnerved, fearing the unnameable something that has leaked into my cabin from this book which I make such poor progress in reading.

Each night as I pick it up before going to bed I find myself having to reread what I had read the night before in order to remind myself of the events which remain, despite the mood of dread, unmemorable, and by the time I have finished reading the portion from the night before I find myself unable to proceed much further, often only a sentence or two, before I drop off to sleep, a sleep which was once untroubled, but which since the taking up of this project of reading the unfinished novel from the previous summer, has been restless, troubled even I should say. I think sometimes that I ought to get rid of this novel, bury it in the woods perhaps or find a local library and put it in the overnight return slot where someone efficient would in the morning figure out what to do with it. But then I reason with myself that this is an absurd way to behave over a novel, especially one I haven't finished and which might, if

I persevere, have a quite rounded and comforting ending, one which would repay all my efforts from last summer and this.

Another possibility would be to take up reading a history of the city in which the central character is located so that in spite of the failure of this particular book I would have nonetheless propelled myself forward. But for some reason this also never happens and again it is evening and I have turned on the lamp and I pick up the novel and open its damp and mildewed pages, pages giving off that vaporish smell of old cabins and foxing. And again the copper moth comes and lands on the top end of the book and again I am filled with the dread of something about to occur, something looming in the distance which I will be unable to fend off, something too vague to get a firm picture of so that I am unable to conceive a plan of attack.

In the morning I wake with the light still on, the book fallen as usual to my chest, and the moth dead and stuck to page 42, the page I have reread any number of times during the course of this particular week. And nothing has yet happened really to the main character, nothing has moved him forward, and he hasn't yet figured anything out. No, he is still doing research and reading in the hopes that one day he will see all things clear, will be able to fall into a damp bed and arise transformed, but as yet he is unable to move beyond p. 42, dependent as he is on my abilities which are for the moment lost, no longer exactly in a swamp of dread, but in the limp sluggishness of being unable to turn to p. 43 on which page it might be that something would finally happen to the main character or that he would finally move beyond the reading stage to something else which he can't quite conceptualize, caught as he is in another's inability to finish the novel which seems vaguely familiar as if I have read it all before.

Where Passion Becomes Sound

George Looney

Touch is redefined each time dolphins make love. The smooth bodies swim for miles together, twirling through water, a dream of what ballet could be without the awkwardness of the human form in gravity, and the water whispers stories that calm each body that swims or floats through it. Even sharks forget their hunger. Because dolphins sacrifice their sleek bodies to passion, sharks do a dance in dark water that could be mistaken for regret, or the longing for sorrow to cling to them like remora. When they rise into water changed by light, where passion becomes sound, the bodies of sharks hum music that's a kind of touch. It's from such moments the stories come, of sharks brushing past the legs of human swimmers. Dolphins spin through water, joined to one another and to the music that touches even the awkward forms of men and women who will tell the story for years of how it must have been a kind of grace that kept the sharks from attacking. Of how warm their bodies were. How gentle the touch.

Oh Never to Have Been
Raymond Federman

Stranded as he is between two moments, between two non-realities, one of which he never thought he would explore, even though fascinated by exotic places, Moinous, rather than look outside of himself to see who he is and where he is going, turns inward, introrse his old friend Sam would say, and launches into a deep self-examination, to see if, once and for all, he can understand himself ...

The first conclusion he reaches, among a number of others, during this moment of self-invasion, if one can permit oneself a little rhetorical contortion, is that even though he may be a good writer, time will tell, as Sam used to say, he is an impossible person, impossible in the literal sense of the word, impossible to understand, just as he finds it impossible to understand himself ...

The second conclusion, an easy one to reach, is that Moinous invented himself, in truth, Moinous says, still in the state of self-invasion, there is no Moinous, Moinous invents himself and cancels himself on the spot of each situation in which he finds himself, he adapts to the circumstances of the moment, positively or negatively doesn't matter since it comes out the same in the end, Sam would surely say, and Moinous must adapt, otherwise he would not be Moinous ...

The third conclusion declares that Moinous conducts his life as a heroic self-construction, though it may appear to others as a pathetic self-deconstruction, Moinous expresses this notion by saying in his head, je vais toujours vers le devenir, Moinous always self-reflects bilingually ...

The fourth conclusion is a conclusion within a conclusion that concludes that Moinous is moving towards an uncertain and precarious becoming, or as Sam once put it, he moves forward in order to fail better...

The fifth conclusion is self-evident, it reveals once and for all that Moinous is violently and incurably self-contradictory, but in the end, as old Sam would certainly emphasize, since everything Moinous says cancels out, he says nothing ...

The sixth conclusion admits openly that Moinous's entire oeuvre was forged out of a confused and chaotic love life, Moinous makes a mental list ...

love given
love denied
love received
love in absentia
love interrupted
love found again
love misdirected
love never found
love lost temporarily
Moinous smiles as he contemplates his mental list lovingly ...

In the seventh conclusion Moinous pauses and wonders if he is prophetic in his work, he shakes his head inside his head, and smiles joyfully at this preposterous thought, and how he has just imagined his head inside his head smiling the smile that smiles at the smile, Moinous digresses back into his next conclusion ...

In the eighth conclusion Moinous thinks that to others he must look very bughouse, as Sam once described William Butler Yeats ...

The ninth conclusion brings Moinous to admit that his position in matters of social behavior is rather unstable, ambivalent, and often unpleasant and irritable, but in political matters, Moinous is unchangeable and constant, he remains a leftist ...

The tenth conclusion digresses to the fact that Moinous was

born left-handed, but became right-handed out of necessity at a young and fragile age because of a fractured left wrist causing him to betray his natural leftist dexterity, and this might explain his perennial crisis of doubt, Moinous approves with a motion of his head inside his head, no smile ...

In the eleventh conclusion Moinous wonders, if to others he appears silly when he tells his stories, Moinous has so many stories to tell, and he loves to tell them, he shrugs his shoulders inside his head, and mumbles, take it or leave it ...

In the twelfth conclusion, Moinous says still shrugging his shoulders, silly perhaps, but unlike the rest of the sillies, as he agrees with himself that his silliness is unique ...

The thirteenth conclusion is important, within Moinous' train of thoughts, for it raises the question of whether or not his life coincides with his work, or vice versa, and if they are part of the same pattern, they must be, Moinous concludes, otherwise, he could not go on living and writing ...

The fourteenth conclusion firmly states that just as Moinous' life is a constant-life-in-progress, his work is also a work-in-progress, Moinous looks pensive as he self-reflects this further and wonders if this means that both his life and his work will always remain unfinished ...

In the fifteenth conclusion Moinous admits that his life is a violent contradiction, but that is in fact the source of his artistic impulse ...

The sixteenth conclusion picks up where the fifteenth conclusion left off, and points out that Moinous' lack of inner self-assurance and his irreducibly divided nature are the dynamics of his writing ...

The seventeenth conclusion brings Moinous to make, in a gentle ironic way, a quick mental list of what obsesses him

... of course the list is incomplete ...

reincarnation
communication
the dead but not necessarily death
artistic medium but not occult medium
supernatural systems
numerology
coincidence
sexuality
lottery
sports

In the eighteenth conclusion Moinous states that he is more interested in human life than vegetal life, though he makes an exception for trees, Moinous loves trees, and if he were to be reincarnated, which he doubts, he would request to come back as a tree, he doesn't know what species of tree he would want to be, but if possible he would prefer to come back as a tall majestic tree on top of a hill ...

The nineteenth conclusion puzzles Moinous but forces him to admit that his thwarted youth, his virile sexuality, his peculiar sentimental association with the happy few, happy fous, as he loves to say, his erotic adventures have lead him to recognize the feminine in him as the source of his creative power ...

In the twentieth conclusion Moinous re-affirms his aesthetics, life is made up of stories, therefore his life is the story of his life, Moinous winks to Moinous in his head ...

In the twenty-first conclusion Moinous asks himself if he is quarrelsome, ruthless, reckless, disrespectful, egocentric, brutal, elitist, then he asks if he is gentle, kind, generous, attentive, caring, interested, polite, he concludes that he is well balanced ...

The twenty-second conclusion raises the question of whether or not Moinous has a tendency to be too verbose, too garrulous, and if his verbosity and garrulousness are screens for his linguistic insecurity and deficiency ...

In the twenty-third conclusion, Moinous congratulates himself for having been able to escape in his writing the cacademic abuse of indeeding, moreovereing, as-it-wereing, thusing, thereforeing, foregrounding, etctering, he also congratulates himself for having managed not to use cumbersome words like redolent, bespeak, purport, adumbrate, insofar as and others he cannot remember now ...

The twenty-fourth conclusion brings a happy glitter to his eyes as he considers how he has managed to avoid in his work the kind of journalistic sentences one encounters too often in bad writing, to illustrate Moinous rereads mentally a sentence in a piece of writing he encountered recently, Yet it is wide of the mark in failing to grasp the tragic import of an excoriating vision of irrevocable action as unelectable destiny, Moinous shakes his head in disgust ...

The twenty-fifth conclusion brings Moinous to ask if his muse has finally spoken to him, or if it is too late, Moinous bangs his fist on the armrest of the seat in which he is seated to do his self-reflecting, and shouts, in his head of course, no, it is not too late, the muse will speak to me ...

The twenty-sixth conclusion is of major importance because it concerns the never ending struggle of the writer, in this case Moinous, to understand from whence the images come that threaten to master him ...

In the second part of this conclusion, Moinous stubbornly considers ways to ensure that these images keep coming, têtu comme une mule, his mother used to say about him ...

The twenty-seventh conclusion brings Moinous to wonder if there is a link between sex and the magic of writing, Moinous does not pursue this thought much further, for he knows that episodes of sexual energy and confusion in his life have always been closely paralleled by periods of magical explosions in his work ...

The twenty-eighth conclusion is briefly stated, irrational humor ...

In the twenty-ninth conclusion Moinous asks himself if he should come down off his stilts more often ...

The thirtieth conclusion consists of another list in which Moinous wonders if he is ...

a compulsive masturbator
a displaced person
a true orphan
un gourmand
un con
a genius
an acrobat
a deranged person
a demented person
a nice person
a fool

Moinous pauses, and then makes a second list in which he asks if he is ...

paranoid
lecherous
shy
crazy
happy
envious
salacious
depressive

In a third list, Moinous loves lists, he wonders if he fears ...

impotence
speechlessness

pain
loneliness
death
obesity
rats & snakes

Moinous asks in the thirty-first conclusion if he would be willing to make a fool of himself to be recognized ... he hesitates ... decides that it is not for him to decide ...

The thirty-first conclusion is enormous in its implication, Am I as I Am, Moinous asks, because my mother forced me to stop loving myself too soon, and as he asks himself this rather intricate question, Moinous, for some unexplainable reason, recalls this line from W.B. Yeats, a shudder in the loin engenders there the broken wall, the burning roof and tower...

The thirty-second conclusion was reached with some apprehension, Moinous questions if his life has been spent vainly in constructing a drama of opposites, anti-selves, masks, metaphors, he who abhors metaphors, Moinous concludes, no, that would be too banal, too much of a simplification, too self-evident ...

The thirty-third conclusion has Moinous worrying about his bones, where will his bones find their final resting place, if they are buried, he wants the skeleton to be buried upright, and if his bones are reduced to ashes, he wants the ashes to be placed in a very tall thin container, Moinous wants to be vertical in death, Moinous bursts into mental laughter ...

In the thirty-fourth conclusion Moinous explains that the past is what one should not have been, the present is what one ought not be, the future is what artists are ...

In the thirty-fifth conclusion Moinous decides that he is a conglomeration of past and present stages of civilization, bits from books and newspapers, scraps of humanity, rags and tatters of clothing patched together as is the human soul ...

Moinous's final conclusion takes the form of a poetic statement, as he remains stranded between two non-realities ...

there in the tomb
the dark will grow darker
and when the wind will come up
from the great void and roar
it will make my old bones rattle

Moinous gets up from his thinking chair and goes directly to his desk to write his conclusions ...

while writing the conclusions he has reached in the process of exploring his inner himself, he stops a moment to reflect further, not about his bones, but about his words ...

Will my words still shake after I have changed tense, will they continue to rattle into history without me, or will there be a sigh of relief from the potentials as they whisper, Moinous, you should not have been, you should have left the dead alone?

Clown
Harold Jaffe

Gacy? I thought you said Bundy.

They nailed Gacy's fat butt in '78.

Got himself 21 life sentences and 12 death sentences.

You know what? He deserved every bit of it.

Executed by lethal injection on May 10, 1994 in Stateville Correctional Center, Joliet, Illinois.

Ring a bell?

Same joint where mass murderer Richard Speck would drop dead of a heart attack in '91.

Speck was a YY dummy who raped then snuffed a bunch of nurses.

That was in '66.

Maybe it was snuff then rape, I don't know.

Speck ended up in pink silk drawers with hormone-induced titties wagging his coated tongue like a bitch in heat.

Gacy was no YY.

John Wayne Gacy was more puke than Duke, a half-ass male from the get-go.

Before zapping him they asked him if he had any final words.

"Yeah, I do. Kiss my ass."

Exit scumbag.

Every exit must have an entrance, right?

Gacy's mom died when he was nine.

Or maybe she didn't die then but was so passive that she might as well have.

His abusive dad was an obsessively macho, borderline psychotic booze-hound.

He called John "Jock" to mock the boy's delicate constitution.

Gacy, a Pisces, got married at 22 to still his own doubts about adequacy.

Became a proud and successful manager of a Kentucky Fried Chicken franchise in Waterloo, Iowa.

Upstanding member of the Junior Chamber of

Commerce.

Honorary Secretary of the Waterloo chapter of Freemasons.

Yo, nothing that good lasts forever.

With two kids of his own, Gacy withdrew his libido from Lucille, his wife, and pursued adolescent boys.

Lucille is also the name of BB King's guitar.

Reckon I ought to introduce myself: My name is Rob.

My mother's name is Roberta.

We come from Roboland.

And we sell rotisseries.

My friends call me Hungsolo.

Gacy called me Hung.

I called him Neck, as in redneck.

Though redneck really didn't do him justice.

I should say here that I ain't a groupie and I ain't a homey.

And you got to know I ain't no homo.

Let's just say I'm captivated by extremity.

Plus I have the cream to pursue my dream.

Made the big $$$ in real estate, same as with Neck.

That's about it as far as what we have in common.

Case you were wondering.

Before prisoner Gacy permitted a visitor he had the wannabe fill out a strict questionnaire.

I wrote I was an ex-lawyer-turned-writer who wanted to recount John Wayne Gacy's story from his own eyes.

Gacy bought the lie.

But what got his juices flowing was my writing I was hung like a horse.

I visited Neck Gacy six times for a total of 23 hours in 1993 and '94 at Menard Correctional Center in Chester, Illinois.

Neck also phoned, faxed and e-mailed me at least a hundred times.

I kept vids, tapes or written records of all of it.

We were tight.

Only he thought we were tighter than I did.

I had severe misgivings about the guy.

Like most serial murderers (mass murderers are different), Neck was a born liar, real slick at it even though he was lumpy and unappealing from a physical standpoint.

The first time I saw him in February 18, 1993 I was struck at how ordinary he looked.

I don't know what I was expecting but he was definitely on the fat side.

About five-seven, 215, with a twisted, upturned nose, wide nostrils and large oily pores.

He had invisible eyebrows, limp colorless hair streaked with grey, two-and-a-half chins, and an infectious grin which made him enormously likeable.

Neck was 100 percent Irish with a hefty dose of blarney.

You can see how he charmed children and adults in or out of his Pogo the clown getup.

Hell, as the Jaycee's "Man of the Year," Neck maneuvered himself into a photo-op with the then First Lady, Rosalyn Carter, both of 'em wearing shit-eating grins.

This was in '77.

After the photo-op he banged her.

True story. Neck balled Rosalyn in the same Chicago suburb tract house where he'd sliced and diced young boys, sprinkled the corpses with quicklime, then lodged them in the crawl space beneath his porch.

Done twenty-five or thirty like that.

Happily, Rosalyn's sinuses were acting up and she couldn't smell the roses.

President Jimmy?

Off in the South Bronx retrofitting tenements in the barrio.

Teaching the poorest of the poor how to pull themselves up by their bootstraps.

I always felt Jimmy should have gotten the Nobel Peace Prize for the hands-on work he did with poor folks instead of Kissinger with his Strangelove posturings.

Here's some of what the cops found in Gacy's Chicago suburb tract house after they nabbed him in December '78 and dug up the bodily remains in the crawl space:

*Eleven porno movies made in Denmark.

*Porno books and magazines with titles such as: *Satan Says **Submit***; *Spread them, Junior*; *The Naked and the Dead*, by Norman Mailer; *I Swallow*; *The Gay Guide to Minneapolis-St. Paul*; and *Men Who Worship Boys*.

*Four hypodermic syringes.

*Six pairs of wrist and leg irons, with keys.

*A twenty foot section of heavy linked chain.

*Thirty-six Polaroid pictures of Pizzerias in the Chicago area.

*Eighteen various sized dildos and butt pugs, several with dried blood and fecal matter.

*A five-year-old wall calendar featuring Disney World in Orlando, Florida.

*Marijuana and rolling paper.

*A wall-mounted pencil sharpener

*Black rubber executioner's hoods, black leather strait jackets, padded rubber blindfolds, chain mail jock straps, and heavy duty Spandex piss gags.

*Two large Mason jars of Snickers and Almond Joy.

Flash forward to '93.

I was living in Omaha, Nebraska, a young and wealthy widower.

Down young bro' comin' straight out of 'Braska.

When visiting condemned killers it was my habit to take the same route and do the same things en route.

Call it ritual, superstition, whatever.

I'd sleep on my left side and in the morning have a bloody mary instead of the usual sectioned grapefruit.

Three-and-a-third spoons of sugar in my coffee instead of four.

Post-breakfast, I used Pepsodent rather than Sensodyne, which was a sacrifice because I have sensitive teeth and gums.

I wore Versace silk thong jocks rather than standard cotton jockeys or boxers.

When visiting the condemned, I traveled with two females, who varied but were always sultry.

Leave Saturday morning, fly my Piper from Omaha

to St Louis, put up there at the Waterfront Hilton and party bigtime Saturday night, always ending with me, my fems, and a couple or three others, male and/or fem, sexing into the wee hours.

Followed by pizza and coffee.

The pizza had to have pepperoni, anchovies and pineapple, the other toppings didn't matter.

Followed by the jacuzzi.

Followed by sleep, the deep drugged sleep of the just.

The waitresses at brunch outside St. Louis would always ask where we were headed and when we told them John Wayne Gacy they would get like all hot and bothered.

Good girls *and* bad are into outlaws. Period.

Call yourself "Kid" and you'll get their attention.

I always reserved a 1993 silver and chocolate Mercedes for the two-and-a-half hour drive to Chester, Illinois.

Had a name for the Benz: Berkowitz. Private joke.

My two female companions were not morning people and were at each other's throats all the way to Chester.

I laughed so hard I peed my jocks.

I don't know about you but I love a cat fight.

Chester, Illinois?

Have you ever shined your brights on rats in a junkyard at two a.m. in the freezing rain?

Maybe take a pop at them with your 12-gauge?

That's Chester, Illinois.

Menard, on the banks of the Mississippi, is an old bleak, brick "correctional center."

You check your metal, get eyeballed, x-rayed, patted down, then meet with your inmate flesh to flesh, though he's cuffed of course.

My two fems would blow kisses at Neck but not go into the visiting area with us till I gave the sign.

I'd be lying if I said Neck didn't make a pass at me the first time he saw me.

He was cuffed, like I said.

We sat facing each other but with no partition.

He was wearing some kind of sweet cologne he must've put on for the occasion.

He tried to rub my bulge with his knee.

After I rebuffed him he grabbed me with his cuffed hands hard around the neck from behind and hissed into my ear:

"I could snap your neck, right now, Puss!"

I was surprised at the power in his arms.

Immediately, two guards burst in, but it was over.

Once Neck said it he seemed to forget it.

He was cool after that.

Well, as cool as John Wayne Gacy can be.

I always brought him stuff: Snickers, Almond Joy, art supplies.

In turn, he let the guards snap photos of him and me and the girls.

Sometimes he brought his newest clown paintings, which he either gave me or sold to me on the cheap.

Pogo the clown grinning in his harlequin garb facing the viewer.

Beneath the smears of bright color you could tell Pogo the clown was Gacy himself, his grin wide as a cut throat.

As art, the stuff sucked.

You know what: I resold a pair of clown paintings to a prestigious
online gallery three or four months ago.

One was an oil, the other acrylic.

Genuine Gacy's.

Fetched me 41 thou.

For the most part Neck and me, we'd talk about ordinary things: home team sports, the nuclear family, encroachment of high technology, the increasing threat of terrorism from the Muslim sector.

Occasionally he turned the conversation to boys, but he'd always catch himself and change the subject.

Once I asked him: "So it gave you pleasure?", referring to 12-year-old Billy Carroll, handcuffed, tortured, sodomized, chloroformed, mutilated, then sprinkled with quicklime and buried in the crawl space.

"Doing Billy Carroll that way gave you pleasure, Neck?"

Neck looked at me hard from beneath his invisible

eyebrows.

Then his mouth got all slack.

I couldn't tell if he was going to laugh or cry?

"What do *you* think?" he said.

What I thought was he was a despicable homo pederast mother-fucking piece of shit.

"I think you're presidential timber," I said.

"If you weren't here in Menard you'd be fartin' around in the Rose Garden.

"Setting policy for the greatest country in the fingerfuckin' free world, Neck."

It was a joke, but Neck didn't buy it.

Just sort of sat there with a weird expression on his face.

I said: "Neck, it's hard to get you to break a smile, but when you put on those Pogo the clown getups, you grin to beat the band.

"And then you go and paint your happy grinning clowns.

"How did you come up with the clown thing, Neck?"

He looked at my eyes to see if I was mocking him.

Finally he said: "I love folks, Hung.

"Specially young folks, adolescent boys and such.

"Love to see 'em happy."

By then it was pushing 4:00 pm, which meant we had to clear out.

That was the law.

The last time I saw Neck alone was five days before his execution.

Which wasn't in Menard but in Stateville, like I said

I pointed to my bulge and let him run the back of his handcuffed hand over it.

Then I backed up and shook my head.

"No more cock.

"You've had it for this lifetime, Neck.

"Think about it in hell."

Those were the last words I said to him.

He phoned me the next morning, but I didn't take the call.

Once upon a time there lived a witch. She was not your usual witch. She was a very contemporary witch; she didn't ride a broom, she drove a vacuum cleaner. She'd gone to therapy. And because eating kids was out of fashion, she now visited them sometimes in their sleep and tickled them till they wet the bed.

At least, that's how kids who were old enough to know better explained things.

So there was this witch. She lived in the woods by a new subdivision. The boys who played baseball were afraid of long fly balls into the trees. The girls who played baseball were all infielders.

Once, a boy and a girl—they weren't siblings, nor were they boyfriend and girlfriend as they were much too young for that—went searching for the witch's house in the woods. They were hoping for candy. They knew the story of Hansel and Gretel and figured a cottage of sweets was worth the risk. They wandered the woods all Saturday. Brambles scratched them. She was a Girl Scout and brought a compass; he brought a bottle of water. Neither of them brought anything to eat as they were going to eat the sugary walls of the cottage, nibble on the house's lintels.

They came home tired, hungry and well past supper. They never saw the witch or her house. They slept all night, deeply. Though they slept in separate rooms in separate houses, they both dreamt the witch visited them in their sleep—she was beautiful: no warts, no straggly hair, and bountiful hazel eyes. She must have had, they both agreed later, a terrific plastic surgeon. When she touched their tummies and the pads of their feet, they chuckled at first and kept laughing till a warmth spread around them, radiating outward, and they awoke in the morning embarrassed and without any good explanation.

Marco Gets Fingered
Peter Conners

Into the bathroom, slowly swaying. Marco lowered his body until the glass door handle was snug in his ass. He pressed it deep. He closed the door. His head was full of boozy vapors masquerading down neural pathways dedicated to perception. The faucet tap receded like a llama neck into vitreous china sink patterns of roosters, pears, and cornflower checkerboards. One man, one toilet. One cocktail bunching table under commingling cherubs in bird of paradise water illusions. Marco jilted the doorknob and took out his thing. This was for urination, but the pink light tinged with red fringe in the corner of the restaurant bathroom made it more than that. A burlesque of Marco. Tango of Marco. Porno Marco. Marco the Snake Charming Pervert. Only problem: alcohol white urine under pink light tinges red. Bloody pee, bad. Even hint of bloody pee bad. The spell broken, Marco scanned the bathroom while his urethra did it.

*

Women keep things in purses. Marco did not know much about them. Some are made of cloth or woven. There is, of course, leather. But he knew they were kept at one's side; slapped into ribs or nuzzled into the curve that famously blushes to hip. They are placed beside chair legs when dining. Luxuriously, they may have a whole seat at the table to themselves. Or they are left in cabs. Stolen by punks running full speed down leafy streets. The sad ones line upper shelves, outdated. His grandmother's snapped like an angry bison (which it wasn't) with a latch that latched. It was full of bad tasting candies and crumpled things. Mentholated misery.

**

It is best when the knock on the door comes after the

beginning of the stream. As it was, Marco spent too much time waiting. There are tricks: reciting the alphabet, counting backwards, eating warm milk, snorting tryptophan. Amino acid. Row row your boat. Trying not to jism.

All the fucking waiting, thought Marco. He called out for the knock-knock person to sit down. Told them to fuck off. Wait. Get lost. Piss off. Marco said, "Yes."

***

"I'm in here," he said.

****

"Sorry," said the other voice.

*****

Marco was not accustomed to restaurants of this magnitude. The city was full of them: dim velvet lighting, burning sage, small mushrooms, everyone, even the ugly ones, in glossy fashion. Marco prided himself on passing them haughtily, even speedily, snootily. Now he was inside the belly licking the smooth bloody walls of muscle and tissue mucus. If the gallery wanted to throw away their money, Marco figured, he'd get a shovel and do his share. Scallops the size of sand dollars. Buckets of red wine. Small fishy eggs, points of toast, mushy dabs of pink and green shit on square white tapestry. Marco guzzled, wolfed, smacked. When he could, he squeezed out potent, disdainful little farts and snickered at the idea of people trying to place or ignore them.

He leaned his head back and looked at the ceiling while the urine flowed. The curly black hair on the back of his neck reached the collar of his sport coat. His head kept tilting. More passed the top of the collar. Then the bottom was obscured; Marco's nostrils gaping wide at the faux-artsy black and white photo of a naked woman's torso hanging over the toilet. Marco tilted, almost tipped. He steadied himself staring ahead at the cursed thing. Like a car or a tree or a bowlful of stingers.

A black and white photo of a bronze sculpture of a real woman bent over the toilet.

******

Marco spat cottony little islands.

****

Before the knock-knock person returned. Before the urine stopped. Before the shivers that made gooseflesh returned to the cortex from whence they came. It was only a matter of time before Charlie and Italo wondered what took Marco so long. Before the alcohol thickened him; permanent broken blood vessels turning his nose to explosion. It was bread mixed with oil. Wine mixed with the bread. Floating sun dried tomato bits in pimento paste. Italo squeezed Charlie's thigh like a loaf of bread. Charlie's oil drizzled Italo's greasy olives. Frowning, always frowning. Yet this fascination was as natural as any bodily function: Marco under the table with his cousin during a family gathering obscured by a table cloth playing the game for which children become famous and ashamed.

Marco knew what might be in there, or not.

Shivers shook from the cortex of the Marco.

****

To dip fingers into the depths or not? Marco scried while washing. The latent possibilities were finite: there would be no solutions. His pupils devoured his conscience, churning it in subterranean rivers with estuaries labeled guilt, possibility, criminal, freedom, ability, milk, willingness, denial, opportunity, reprisal, each offshoot a new twitch on Marco's otherwise oily, wrinkle free visage. The decision, really, was made before fly reached apex. Masquerade was folderol. Marco. Drunk and evil. Sneered. At himself. He enjoyed this darkness embodied in the little black purse that even a wharf rat could recognize as designer of one stripe or another.

****

When Marco was a boy he was sometimes a bad little boy. He enjoyed making marks. He marked the garage with a pencil alphabet the length of a diesel station wagon. The b reversed. The worst, the thing that really marked Marco as bad, was lipstick destruction. Marco pulled bullet tubes from his mother's purse, twisted them, cap closed, until the lipstick reached the top and kept twisting until the shapely conical edge smashed flat. This ruined lipstick. Cost money. Shed tears.

****

Marco, to this day, is intimidated by lipstick.

****

Saliva neutralized by red wine. Marco's mouth was the Kit-Kat Lounge: slightly overripe strippers schmoozed sexagenarians on coarse animal pelt sofas across the ridge of his gums; they sashayed down the runway of his tongue trailing frayed boas. Marco felt stiletto heels twang nerve ends. Dense unfilled cavities pickled in red wine stewed in putrescence. Marco plucked out the golden foil, unwrapped the caramel. Thick molten toffee spread. Marco pushed it against the roof of his mouth to hasten flavor into his echo chamber head. He crinkled up the wrinkly.

****

Here is a phone number here is a phone. Here is something Marco does not possess: a cellular phone, a phone that functions at the cellular level. No creased phone numbers have been passed into his hand for two years. There aren't matchbooks with tiny little phone numbers and tiny little names like "Deena" "Sharon" "Ellie." Mangled napkins with redundant establishment names dug out of his pockets at 3 a.m., tossed onto his nightstand amidst disinterred flecks of chemicalized tobacco.

****

All the world was swearing at Marco. Two people swore at Marco. Others were perhaps thinking of swearing at Marco. Which is, sometimes, but not usually, as bad as swearing at Marco.

Marco removed it in front of the mirror and side-shifted in front of the toilet. Who knew there was urine in the bladder? There was urine on the toilet seat before it went into the toilet.

Droplets?

****

Bloody ringlets?

****

The device was inserted to staunch the flow of blood from moon time. Marco playfully chewed the end of his pretend cigar, shifting the waxy tubular paper from cheek to cheek. Tasted like shelf.

These were days of experimentation for Marco. He unwrapped the tube turned on the tap to the faintest of trickles to the lightest tickle of a trickle to the dribblingest trickling tickling and tested the flow it could hold.

****

Hard to walk with it up there.

****

Marco wore a severed plastic finger with an insertion point of red blood over his index finger too long after Halloween. It didn't match the costume, but the severed finger fit well. It hugged his index like a second skin. It was not overtly funny. That passed naturally with the season. But in a smug way, in the way of having a finger that someone else may not possess; Marco had eleven fingers. His choice whether to have the new eleven or the usual ten. He often chose eleven. He would not relent to ten for a spell: the kernel of the Marco of the independent artist. Resisting the barrage of the ten fingers.

There was blood even crusted into the grottoes of the knuckles.

****

Treachery?

****

The severed finger lay in the purse like a slippery little tongue in an empty stomach. The finger was dedigitized. Nine fingers swayed alone like sea kelp. Real finger rubberized. Marco and the ragged knuckle incision. Marco held the dead finger beside his live fingers ascertaining its original pecking order: down the line to the thumb to the pinkie. Naughty American finger. Big fat chief. Marco swore at Marco with the American bad finger pointed at Marco.

****

It was a question to which Marco desired no answer.

Araby
Joyelle McSweeney

The chaise lounge peers down the slope where the last nuns in L.A. move on footpaths among the cacti, squirrel-grey as the hand Dawn lays across her belly. Pregnant with repose. Dawn seals the wound with a glowing finger then lifts it to her lips. For silence or to puff-puff the smoke. Cool ellipse, the burning taper. Her cloche-hat dips past its axis. She edits the slope steep as an early morning run at perspective, nature just awakened, man not yet knowing how to look. The nuns' cramped bodies like allegorical boulders point to themselves or the desert: look.

Once a boy genius could render a rabbit in thousands of minute strokes, turn them over into image; today we could tally them up. Today the girl genius paints big dripping swirls of hue and the arched forms of rabbits pulling the belly of the field apart as the rabbit is torn by beagles or the book is read to pieces. The book of my captivity; I read it apart. I read it till the pieces fell like tears in my lap and I slumped with my sisters in the pew.

The latest journeymen are pornographers of scale. Planes, wax candles, steths, pulmonary tubes, plumblines, dozers and cranes. They make a barn from the belly of a whale. They make a Fellini overview, an encyclopedic strain. In the auctionhouse of lovers, these contort to slip a splinter from the paw, a finger into the lips. The pope issues an encyclical on the use of double imagery; his own name means potato or plague. The news reels on the freeway, the resistance sloshes like water in the arms of a child holding an aquarium. He learns to see through the spray and walk while crying. He arrives with a dry tank.

In the real country, the straw hat smiles dimly on its calendar of fields. In repose. Now sheltering in the barn: the scout, wench, prostitute, and dentist. The scent and the prickly feel. The vertiginous ladder, the model horse. The nun, soldier, and the child hacker. The cable modem maundering and blinking like an eddy veteran. Two bicycle wheels round with surprise and fear. Two eyes pounded with spokes like the goldfish the Surrealists kept on hand to slice or turn tricks through. Sir Mouse the Cat, the matinee idol.

> ITEM: The country mouse met the city mouse at a hand jive competition. Palm to palm, they split the scene and were never parted, as Minnie Mouse made a blue cartoon with the bubblegum pop star, the blue-skinned candywrapper. Follie a deux with the wit and the rapier. One actress in all the roles.

The hour was at last an autoclave for the indigo and the vertigo for the guilt already forgiven, prenom 'white.' For the white instep of the cow's ribs hanging from the rafter. The last nuns in Stockholm were imported with promises of local taste and health care. A Polisk: Eine Kleine Mienie Moe. Which game taught the inmates of the kindergarten the false premise of difference. The strap dangling the books. The string knotted around the slate. The revolving light. The potted bellies. The two flags knotted in embrace.

But the chaise lounge was a model of forgiveness. Its polished ankles were always cool despite their rich hue which was a metonym for fire. This made one dream of the false fires the sailors built altars to, first aligning them with the true faith of home. The mast lining up, then dipping, then respun. Steady on, men. In the dream these fires were all of the same quality: false. Comparison was mute as a novice. The bulletin spun in the chambers, the chambers spun around. The pinwheels painted onto the gravestones spun on their Nazi axes.

Click.

The actual forgiveness was aquamarine and embroidered with a hydra of dandelion floss which seemed to flex as one gazed at the space where the figure should be. The apartment had a large central slot and a choir of shutes and vents. The room was cool as post-contamination unit, the refrigerated saferoom in the grade school locked in the groove of the empty track. The body laid out for the bag or the bandit.

The degrading solace of the sea.

Click.

There the hydra stuck up its flowing head and offered to filter, a neat barrier between life and death. These barriers were so multiple, so multiple and all over, and often occupying the same time in place. The philosopher gathered the complicated skirts of this thought around him and started up the steps. All the girls stood in the race with wet ankles and dripping baskets. All the girls wore the hydra-logos on their shoulders and shoulderbags and as they nursed through the footraffic the benthic life that summer seemed to glow and redouble.

Click.

The pristine cervix was scraped, the yards were scraped and sprayed to a Cartesian wellness, but motors and fumes gunked up all the other organs of sense. What god would try so poorly to disguise hisself? For a god must have a sex. At night the actors gathered in the caps that identified them as workers, in the redface that identified them as Indians, dunking sugar into the tea. In the sneers that identified them as students. In the promotional CD. In the totaled channel full of shopping carts and rapiers and muck. A force that disguises itself as all things may not be recognized, or only like a glint in the harbor, a spark in the eye. Take your oysterknife and distinguish it. An earl of great price.

Click

It is a torrent without oceans, a torment without names. It is a self-serving missile, a dues-seeking club. It involutes and you may safely ignore it. You may safely brush it off. Wrapped in your sunburst blanket on the chaise. At night the city ripples under the plate there is no need to drape on account of its height. Nothing could peek in but ozone, and that notorious vacuity could carry no tale away. Poor dome-crushed cupbearer. It staggers down the slope.

Capturing the Shadow Puppets
Derek White

Even though I didn't understand their customs, I was initiated into a tribe in Indonesia called the *Wayang Gulick*. We lived on plains peppered with the occasional Bodhi tree. It started to rain, which was our cue to catch wild gods. The rest of the tribe had enough experience to know that whenever it rained, the gods took shelter under the trees. We huddled in our mud hunting huts until the rain had built up to a steady downpour.

All at once we ran out to capture the gods, chanting and zig-zagging to disorient them. It was hard to catch the gods as they were invisible. The other tribe members knew from experience where they would be. I just had to trust they knew what they were doing. My mentor, Nyoman, caught a baby god with ease. Following his example, I took my large bath towel and threw it at a sheltered spot under a tree. When I jumped on the towel I felt the god squirm under it, surprising even myself. "Good catch," said Nyoman, handing me a flour sack. "Put it here. Come Wednesday you can sell it in the town market for ten thousand rupees—enough to live on until the next storm."

We brought the gods back to Nyoman's ceremonial hut. My luggage was in the corner, still packed and tagged with customs chalk. It crossed my mind to sneak the god into my bag, but Nyoman directed me to let it loose. The walls of this ceremonial weren't in place yet. It was constructed with four pine masts and a palm thatched roof. I was reluctant to let my god loose, but Nyoman assured me the walls would rise. Nyoman had rigged the thatched ceiling with mirrors and an electrical current running clockwise in a square loop to give the optical illusion of four walls, tricking the gods into thinking they were caged. I disagreed with him on the principles of physics. This went against everything I had learned up to this point.

Nyoman was disappointed in me. He yelled up to his wife for backup. This was a matriarchal society and Nyoman got most of his knowledge from his wife. She agreed it was true without showing her face. We could hear her talking from somewhere in the loft of the hut. I was curious to see what else she was doing up there. Then she commented out of the blue that whenever she heard an intruder come in, she stuck a paperclip in the electrical socket. Nyoman admitted that they had the wiring in place, but didn't have electricity yet.

I heard a noise behind me that sounded like a baby gasping for its first breath. I turned and saw an open door with the latch hanging, still swinging and squeaking. The door was embedded in a wall that wasn't there before. The gods had escaped because I had tried too hard to understand their customs.

Self-Portrait with Apologia
Brian Johnson

The prophets said, "There is a time for this kind of love, and a time for that. A time for The Magic Flute, a time for Deep Throat." If I mistake the time, please, stay with me. I am still a young man. You should never drop a young man, as you would never slap an old man. We are both confused, and confusion leads to curious fantasies, and curious fantasies to strange acts. Listen, please: I mistook my two loves. I mingled them, as one mingles Latin and Anglo Saxon in a graveyard. I am still as tall as ever, as muscular, as brilliant as you wish. And if I emerge a polished husband, the rough Viking hangs in the closet, furry-as-a-dog, ready to shake at your command. Your man Monday is not your man Friday, and we're all a species of harebrained Lear, wandering the face of the earth, asking his subjects, "Who is it that can tell me who I am?" Melancholia gives way to Saturnalia, and Saturnalia drives toward Bacchanalia, where the very concept of risk melts away. Still, by the end of the night, Melancholia returns. The most festive of operas has a dark coloring, similar to the men in black at a garden party. The hats are so cheerful, the audience may be misled. Your breasts meanwhile cast a spell, and swell, almost big enough to lift me. I enjoy your legs. There is a time for that, a little clearing in the woods, a sunspot, a capsule in the gloom, which gets me thinking my being can become something else, something happier and lighter, as if my planetary influence were flight and not these footprints. The lift-off is temporary. The rain keeps falling, at various speeds, with various thicknesses, some of them nearly unbearable, and I am huddled at the foot of a tree, wanting you to lift me, wanting you to go away. Such a bare, forked animal I am, and somehow lost, thrown off the path. There are degrees of nakedness. I am still a young man, an actor of manhood, in fact, and I cannot say which degree of nakedness is suitable for the occasion. I would compose myself, if I knew how. I would be more elevated, or more plain, give you more art or less hope. You suspect, perhaps, that mine is a hopeless case.

You can purloin me and get nowhere. It's not me. In person, and on paper, none of my confessions stand up to the flesh. I am full of wishes that do not recognize each other, of moods that come from different spirits. I wear motley, and good will never come of motley. I mistake what I'm feeling as I mistake what you're feeling, which leaves us forever in the dark, befuddled or rapturous, but never at peace. It may be that the slit in your sarong and the slit in my cape are all we know, and cannot tell, of marriage.

The Underpants Tree

Alice Hoover angrily wonders how an eighty year old woman, chronically underweight for her entire life, can suddenly fail to squeeze her belly into a pair of size 22 mail-order underpants. It can only mean one thing: she is pregnant. *How ridiculous!* The three-packs of size 20, size 18, and size 16 are all in the bathroom garbage can. In a rage, she rips off the size 22s, shoves open the window, and heaves them through the darkness like a fiery comet.

It is 1:00 a.m. on a moist and silvery August night. Topless, and now briefless, poor, tired, hot, pregnant Alice leans her elbows against the windowsill to follow the trajectory of her underpants. They streak across the yard, brilliant as a UFO. Amazingly, they land in her neighbor's maple, the twin to her own, and dangle precariously in the lunar glow. The open leg holes look like screaming mouths. Alice opens her own mouth wide enough to scream, but shrieks silently. She feels like she could eat that fat old moon, tear into it with her fierce teeth. In fact, she looks like she has; her pearlescent stomach is huge, a rival to Earth's satellite, trapped in the pathetic orbit of her tiny house. She wonders if this miracle pregnancy will result in a multiple birth, then pictures the contortions she will have to practice to nurse a litter of mewling newborns.

Poetry in the Sky

Alban Kirby writes poems of love on three foot lengths of pale blue ribbon. With bottles of Wite-Out, he paints lines using the words cherish, angel and starshine in radiant white calligraphy. He plans to tie his poetry on the branches of the towering maple outside Alice's second floor bedroom window, directly across the way. He imagines her delighted face when she finds his words floating like puffy clouds on their blue satin skies in the morning light.

From his desk, Alban gazes at the pair of size 22 white cotton woman's briefs perched like a tropical blossom on the branch outside his bedroom window. *They must be a message of love, tossed across the narrow yard like a rare orchid, fragrant and alluring.* He is unworthy of the wearer, but he imagines her delicate fingers flinging this bloom straight toward his heart. He tries to reach the moonlit panties from his desk, but he can't quite grasp the elastic waistband. He attempts snaring them with his ruler, but they tangle in the twigs. Fearful of the long drop to the dark ground, Alban decides to admire them from afar, perfect and nearly attainable— like the lovely Alice herself, Alice of the platinum ringlets, Alice of the white silk dressing gown.

Angel with a Weapon

Beneath Alice's window, a shadowy form approaches through the leaves. She looks down and sees Alban struggling to climb her maple, a bouquet of ribbons waving in one fist. He ascends slowly, smiling, totally unaware of his naked observer. Alice watches in horror as Alban reaches the level of her window and begins to knot his streamers around her branches.

Her scream finally emerges as an ear-splitting, rage-filled question: "What the *hell* are you doing, you little moon-faced alien? You hairless, crater-skinned, fish-lipped freak!"

Blindly, she reaches behind herself for a weapon, until her hand locates the hose of the vacuum cleaner and she lets Alban have it full in the face. For a moment Alban continues to stare at his angel in all her moonlit glory. He balances on the branch like a huge white bird with blue satin plumes, then plummets earthward, wingless, through the maple's outstretched arms.

The Orange Mummy

As Alice leans over the sill to watch his descent, her ponderous abdomen pulls her forward into the night. Breasts flapping like useless wings, she falls, landing right next to her admirer, her skinny limbs at odd angles on the damp lawn. Her arm brushes across Alban's oily chin and ends up resting on the top of his head. *Surely I have murdered this tree-climbing juvenile delinquent.* She pokes his eyelids with her good hand, but they remain closed.

Suddenly, Alice is aware of her aged nudity. She reaches desperately for the orange tarp protecting the stack of firewood next to the garage. With one hand she wraps the mildewed plastic around her torso, then struggles to stand. Two fingers curve strangely backward on the other hand, and her nose is bleeding. But her legs are working, so she gets up and looks down at the sprawled intruder.

Alban is perfectly still. Despite cheeks cratered with acne, his forehead and scalp are as smooth as a dome of delicately veined marble. *Just look at the size of that head!* His protuberant eyelids and large lips give him an odd, froglike appearance. Long, elegant fingers emerge from his silver cuffs. While Alice holds her breath, Alban flutters his eyelids, revealing opal irises with wide black pupils.

Alban is stunned by the vision of Alice, wrapped like an orange mummy, leaning over him and dripping blood from her nostrils onto his sparkling shirt. *My darling even bleeds in two perfect lines of rubies, jewels that dazzle as they fall.* Her frizzy hair rises in a wild gray mushroom cloud, but to Alban it is a starlit silver halo. *Did she really greet me in the heavenly treetops in a pure and unclothed state? Before I fell, was Alice tossing me a rope so I could climb up to her window?* Thankful, blessed by the love of an angel, he reaches up to touch the hem of her flowing gown.

Silver Tadpoles

As his fingertips make contact with the clammy tarp, Alice experiences the shock of her first contraction. *Oh Lord, I am going to give birth to my magic little Dionnes right here, in front of this dazed nutcase, flopped on his back like a metallic turtle.* Again, she collapses, crumpling inside her plastic tent, her belly as hard as a boulder. Annoyed, she wipes her bleeding nose with her good hand and whimpers. Her water breaks and pools beneath the quaking maples. Before she loses consciousness, the last thing she sees is Alban Kirby, *that tinsel-eyed dodo*, staring up her tarp.

A tearing pain awakens her to the sound of Alban shouting, "*Push!* I can see another head!" He tries to capture what appears to be a hovering, silver tadpole with enormous egg-shaped eyes. Three other human polliwogs follow a beam of light to a lozenge-shaped hole in the sky. *My babies!* The last child emerges in a shower of sparks, wet and wide-eyed, staring into Alice's face with intense awareness. He has a broad searching mouth covered with gold flecks, and little reaching hands in two rows down his chest. Alice tries to catch the infant, but he levitates above her palms, then joins his siblings in their journey across the sky.

Alban reaches out and picks up two fallen blue ribbons. He gently ties them in bows around her ankles, then rubs her cold toes between his hands. Alice lies on her back in her sticky tarp in her strange backyard, looking up at where her miracle quints have vanished, zipped up in the twinkling night like five lost stars.

An Underground Constellation

Alice notes that her position is perfect for stargazing, but then glimpses the placenta, glowing like a jellyfish in the moonlight, a separate universe, its sparkling tentacles waving, beckoning. Countless miniature spheres, like amphibian eggs in a congealed inner mass, bubble anxiously, awaiting attention. Alice stands up slowly, then turns her back. *No!*

"Good-bye, you albino tree frog pervert. No more. It's over!" Alice struggles, limping, to her back door, her blue ribbons dragging like meteor trails. "Go home!" She does not glance back at Alban Kirby. Not once.

Riveted, Alban watches her leave. Once the door is shut and locked behind her, he immediately takes a slender metal vial from his shirt pocket and pours the bright, hissing contents into his hand. Panting softly, he begins to plant thousands of chrome seeds in the moist ground where the tarp had sheltered his love. Fine, thirsty roots are already emerging as Alban pats the fragrant earth in place. Like a Portuguese man-of-war, the placenta glides over the fertile soil, releasing eggs to merge with the sprouting seeds. Then it sinks into the teeming ground, absorbed like summer rain.

Quietly, Alban unhinges the polished dome of his scalp and reaches behind his eyes to lift out his iridescent brain. He places it on the awakening soil. Pulsating vessels descend from his brain like pewter hoses, spouting blinding light. He lets his life run out in rivulets of brilliance, down into his sacred garden. There it flows to feed the planted constellation of his hungry, star-eyed children, the true reason for his visit to Earth, for his one hundred year residency in an eighteen year old body, adolescent flesh guided by hormones. He is exhausted, extinguished by interplanetary passion and obsessive love.

Blue Light, Silver Light

Alice's quints are merely decoys, drones, guides for the subterranean generation. Alice herself is only an emptied earthling vessel, the unwitting donor of womb, placenta, and chromosomes to another planet. Poor, senile Alice, now useless, shrinks smaller and smaller, alone forevermore in her cramped bedroom. She fades into the otherworldly blue light of her TV, her only comfort the faithful vacuum cleaner glistening at her side.

And Alban, now hollowed and still, sleeps eternally against the gurgling earth. His offspring busily suckle at the roots of the mighty trees, gaining green strength from the heart of the pulsing planet. In a year they will emerge with hybrid souls, botanic and zoologic vigor united in a constellation of super beings. These sylvan titans will depart on a path of silver light to repopulate Alban's waiting planet.

Cruel Illumination

Now, ecstatically sighing, the twin maples link hands over Alban's bowed, open head, shielding his empty shell from the cruel illumination of the moon. Their crossbred descendants nestle safely in the soil among the roots, pressing their greedy mouths to the flowing veins of the contracting planet.

The Amityville Horror
Arielle Greenberg

Hey, Eloquence. Stardust. —— all about the common currency. Without the gold —— just a girl who is equivalent of tending. Soft-soap. Remember?

—— alone in the brass library. A bit of art: pagan, womanly. —— plan on magic. Look it up in the card catalog. Under a man's name. —— haunted? —— hope.

Don't eat the meat of animals —— swear to love. —— — live by the house of horrors, of swimming pools; by the synagogue (—— for a short while belong. —— light modernist flame-buttons for kaddish, the sorry dead. —— of toilet, the powder room, taffeta dress.); by the cemetery.

One night —— walked until night was gone, a neighborhood of very new houses. Was this the same silver street? —— didn't fear —— soprano, or the abnormal smear of —— lynched sex, but —— father drove —— — home in a scotch glass and this was alien. —— sat in —— stomach.

The second poem for ——. Maybe the third.

So suburban. At a loss for articles. Gendered out by sprinklers, fine gram chemicals seeding & receding. All a sparkle. Ballerina. Vanity.

Eat —— heart out. —— watch the movie about the toolshed, about Jesus, about vomit. Things have gone too far, lack of sleep. —— religion is a velvet cloak someone else will sew for —— to wear to the rape fair. —— body-painted. Years of assholes. Currency, remember gold? Celebrity?

—— tend to not believe in —— anymore until ——

pass ———— house with the vacant camper and think of the Christmas tree ———— mother made, and ————, the woods of ————, pores, some Hawaiian perfume in a pot ———— mentioned before, the plastic chain ———— once wore taped to a black satin shirt, another girl wore a riding hat with a black veil, ———— contacted the doors through a Ouija board, the times ———— made fudge, undone now, drained.

The Work of Art as Seen from Barnard's Star
Dimitri Anastasopoulos

*E*nds: Make a long story short.
Means: Observe earth's laws, links between objects, from a distant planet.
Rematerialization: On the streets of Buffalo on a late March afternoon just before dawn.
Travel Speed: Three angstroms per second.
Form: A report about humankind.

> At the entrance to the Hotel Iroquois icicles hang from the canopy then drip onto stone slabs where the water turns to ice again. Welcome.
> Water freezes and when it's free it finds the path of least resistance. It doesn't float, as bird feathers float, it doesn't flutter, as cereal flakes flutter atop the oat silos by the harbor.

Impression: Empty streets and the threat of liberty, darkness beyond dim streetlamps.

> Blood in the snow at the foot of a revolving door.
> A hotel hallway. A door opens to a suite. Curtains partially cover painted vistas of bygone eras.
> Now leaving public space and entering a private one. A space fashioned by the inhabitant. Not by communal laws.
> The room is empty. Upstairs the floorboards creak. Footsteps.
> Panic deserts the rabbit as it dives into its hole.
> A white-clad figure limps down the stairs. She is breathing heavily. The smell of her limbs: citronella, hairspray, decaying skin.

The Evolution of Illness: Ear plugs worn to bed, cotton in nostrils, a black mask over the eyes. A mosquito net covers the face and torso, a plastic jumpsuit like that of an ancient astronaut.

> Her body disrobes and slides into the clawfoot bathtub,

her white, white skin.

This is why the Buffalo rose is a flower that requires worship.

A change in the air, a desperate need to protect life.

This is why astute and practical readers prefer works of non-fiction.

The absence of words supports the idea that life is harmonious. Speech burdens the new existence.

This is why soundtracks of babies babbling are laid over instrumental music in popular songs.

Need bleeds into the white-clad woman's hotel-bound life. If allowed to flourish, need will bring her companionship and love.

The passage from one feeling to the next is a delicate one.

There is almost no solution.

The last thing she wants is generosity. That is worse than loneliness, worse than need. She wants others to suffer from need at least as badly as she does. It has to be "at least" as bad.

This is why no one is ever lonely on the tundra. This is why igloos stay warm.

History: The hotel is built in a space that always awaits her arrival and departure. The plot of land is a kind of freedom. Space is a form of freedom.

Human Narrative in the Form of Commandments: 1. Never put dwelling in the hands of an architect. 2. There are many free elements at play. 3. The nature of space has to be heeded. 4. Between any two given bodies, there is ample space. 5. Hotel rooms accord with the spaces already given. 6. Above all else, the location of the hotel and the city and the star and the galaxy is paramount. 7. A location anticipates space, and for this purpose the open plot of land in this city is perfect.

Shadows on the wainscoting in the room.

The wood floor is bordered by a Greek key design of alternating dark and light brown shades. As the room grows older, it shows evidence of scuffs and grooves: the ravages of human habits. The room forms itself around these facts. Anyone who breaks this harmony is an intruder.

Primitive drawings on the wall in crayon.

This artwork is not for sale. It is secret work, a whisper out of earshot, a heart that never forgives. It is an idea of a thing projected from the mind of a primitive onto the craggy surface of a plaster wall. An anteater between the legs of a boy, the sun rising from a river, a hunter without a head, a tree growing out of his torso, giant fire ants devouring a moon that has sprouted arms.

Into the mythic moment when a human first forged an image of the world around him.

Into a time before abstract meaning: when man first discovered his ability to think apart from things, by incarnating as objects the very movement of his thoughts. Something primal and scarcely human. This is terror and the all-seeing eye. This is simplicity, clarity. The very opposite of the abstract, it is the enemy of enigmas everywhere.

The sun rising from a river is at the very origin of being.

Human organs, brains, and spirits spill out into the universe and become the very things they are separate from.

The universe is the not-me. The struggle against the universe.

Even the cruelest death is no more significant than cutting off a head of cabbage.

Humans have the freedom of a decapitated head.

Laughter is a fact of city life. But it is hard to hear.

To think of objects in general without imagining them in particular is possible in this city.

Narcolepsy persists.

Buffalo is a space between life and death.

This is a kind of hope. It relies on the repetition of the If.

The primitive drawings on the wall are illuminated by the various lights of day.

It is difficult not to be bothered by ideas which make sense only in dreams.

Symbolic things bother humans a great deal.

In dreams, all symbols vanish.

Mission: Sweep away the old life and the risk of the new. "New" in the sense of the new day. New in the sense of time passing, of a life yet to live, of things yet to see.

The woman in white begins her slow ascension to a floor above.

In the center of the primitive wall there is a door to a smaller room. That door opens.

An enormous steel sculpture occupies all of the room's limited space.

Shunts of steel proliferate at all angles, an elbow here, a backward thrust there, three fingers shoot from one limb, three nubs from another: black density at the sculpture's center. Geometry, abstract rods on a canvas, flagella under the eyelids: nothing real.

Strings of dried roses hang upside down from their stems.

Frost vapors rise from the hollow steel cage at the center which is raw and vulnerable like a punctured lung.

This is why human corpses are cremated and tossed to the heavens.

This is why cars speed at night on vibrating freeways.

This is why a mammal refuses food and lays down to die when a virus replicates inside it.

This is why men drink from streams but not from oceans.

This is why the earth quakes when the sky breaks open a storm.

Because of a room filled with steel the human heart knows mortality and the finite beating of each chamber.

Because the room cuts off the blood from running into each steel limb. It is a space occupied by sculpture that ends the possibility of space and thus possibility itself.

A new microcosm. One that casts off mute realizations, the profundity of innocent thoughts: the work of an ant is the ant itself. Nothing else.

In this city, there's no interpretation or analysis: never the words "this means that."

Facts are materials that insist on a communal reality. Absent of facts, the human body simulates an existence which knocks it out of harmony with its surroundings.

Visual Sensors Off: Touch communicates not only the chill of the steel and the moisture collecting in the ridges of its surface, but something else.

This is why art is best viewed from a distance.
Each steel limb betrays a trace of its human creator.
This is why a toilet is a work of art.
A tiny cage at the sculpture's precise center. Inside, a spongy, wet, fibrous organ that both engulfs and resists.
A human heart. The taste of blood and rust.
A secret access into the sculpture: it isn't booby-trapped. When a work is composed, the creator must account for his own body within the work. A space remains. The work is constructed around this body.
Access is granted only to those who press against flesh.
The myth of the new human race, the true story told, echoes of an event forgotten and forbidden mention for over a decade.
The heart is an emblem that contains this story of a people who were here once, on this earth.
It requires time and demands blood.
A strange joy rises when pressing into the sponge flesh, a sickly lament wells up in the room. Not from morbid desire, not from an all too generic compulsion for the real.
This is why men and women go naked in the cold.
The hotel owners not only lose a room, but gain a reputation as a house of murder and art.
It is a monstrosity. An intimidator, it occupies almost all its space, and refuses to let the observer see it totally. At its heart is a secret.
This is why you should never stare directly into the sun.
The room is silent, the hallway is silent. The city is silent.

Hunt Mountain
Alison Townsend

(in memory of Michael Wittreich, 1951-2001)

When the night my stepbrother put his wrists through the window became the summer we had to hide all the sharp objects in the house—knives with their glittering edges, razors, glass which could be shattered, ready to cut—we kids took to walking the mountain. Each evening after supper when fireflies kindled the air like sparks of cool lightning, we met, without plan, at the foot of the driveway, the white gate open on the road before us, the blue pines bleeding slowly into dusk.

Purposeless at first, sauntering past the neighbors', we moved slowly together, drifting along in August's inertia. Past the house where Mr Ranier stood, dour in gray farmer's clothing, his wife motionless on the porch swing beside him. Past the crazy Mahoneys'. Past Miss Keeler's, landlady and local patron of the arts, where twin pugs barked frantically behind a picket fence. Past it all we strode, and away from our own home, leaving behind the place where my father sat brooding—pipe smoke wreathing the patio—and my stepmother's rage sizzled, sucking air from each room until breath itself felt like glass breaking.

Bickering, trading insults over our shoulders, we filled the air with conspiratorial humming until someone—maybe my stepbrother—said, *Let's go somewhere! Let's go somewhere now!* while Holsteins paused alongside in the meadow, listened, then lowered their heads to the grass. We picked up speed as we left house lights behind us. The road turned from black-top to hardscrabble under our sneakers. We walked fast, the Queen Anne's lace as high as our shoulders, the ordinary world of stone walls and upland meadows another country dreaming itself into being. Blackberries gleamed. A fox yipped an inscrutable love song. Mountain laurel lifted bundles of white fire to the sky. My stepbrother led.

We followed, panting, the road a white path that pulled us upward to the sandy patch marked for picnics and parking.

We never stayed at the top long—there was nothing to do there—but crashed through the tangle of sumac and wild grape to a flat rock, our secret lookout over the curve of the valley. Far below lay the farms, studding the fields like fires set against night's arrival; the Titicus River, silver and slow in the marshlands; and our own house, grown minute and diminished. We felt so small, looking down on the lights. Home seemed so distant that we looked at one another and without a word began running, the real reason for climbing the mountain the pleasure of our descent.

Plunging from forest to field, we ran, sometimes paired, sometimes singly, crazed with momentum and the heat of our bodies, each one a boomerang arcing homeward. Our hearts rattled in our chests like rocks on the mountain, its granite outline glazed by the rising moon. Faster and faster we spun, our feet whirling like pinwheels. We leapt stone walls, avoided cow pats and thistles, twisted ankles and continued, unable to stop, each one racing the dark and the others, determined to be first one to set foot on the road.

And then we were there, the house floating like a lit ship before us. We crossed the road, clattered up the porch steps without speaking. Our thoughts were on ice cream and the shape of our own beds, and my stepbrother was laughing, The screen door banged. Moths rippled in eddies behind us. We went in, moving from darkness into a strangely light world—as if it were a safe place that we entered. As if there were no memory of blood upon glass there.

You Just Keep Going (Tong'Len #1)
Ethan Paquin

You just keep going steady like the sloop on Buzzard's Bay I never did see though I spent decades of leaning over the railings to see it, dropped quarters into the binoculars countless times

you just keep going I stepped out of the shower thinking too much, as I usually do when stepping out of the shower, realizing my life will be perfectly symmetrical on September 16, 2005 (I was born March 16, 1975 = 30 years –> March is 3 months into the year so subtract 3 from 12 for balance's sake = September)

you just keep going so let me keep going with my explanation – so she took this pear and it was shaped like one half of her torso, one side of hip and it was very pretty but I'm too slow

you just keep going while the building keeps sagging, building I dreamt about one October back in grad school, maybe one incorporated into an old poem draft likely never taken too seriously

you just keep going but maybe the neighbor does not, for he wonders how to build a metallic egg. I was once a chauffeur for the stars I was once a little kid-minion for the chicken farmer man

you just keep going and so does night, slow wheels and soda can fizz

you just keep going, all the things your kids say you meant to record but forgot

you just keep going, but the seascape that made such a vast impression on you doesn't give anything to you that's able to be stored in a tiny box under the trundle you just keep going to the farm atop the hill because you think maybe someday you'll bump into the adolescent boy and girl Homer painted in A Temperance Meeting

you just keep going and a cryin and a feelin she won't touch you in the woods like she used to – Kinsman Creek cold and beautiful falls off the west

you just keep going buoys, you just keep on because the ships all need you

you just keep going grasses, aimless and up and always if only for the sun, you just keep on going never stopping

when I say you just keep going I think everyone out there need listen
      to the sound of your feet shuffling in beautiful leaves

This Is the Beginning of Time
Sherrie Flick

The city streets are slick and flat and the idea of living in the middle of a big, empty patch of nothing is everywhere around me. I'm thirsty. Even after four whiskies, even after two glasses of wine. I raise my finger. The bartender looks away.

And then time stops. Like a pancake; like black coffee; like the darkest night, the windiest street and no streetlights; like you leaving. Just like that. Like the cord in the subway car.

I finger the dirty cord, watch it stretched taut—vibrating, wondering.

There is a kind of logic to flatness—to this flat place—that escapes the rest of the bumpy world. Even the most complex combination of dilemmas becomes easy, a grid. A map anyone could read. Join in. That's all they require.

And still, I don't—or can't. And still, here I am. Waiting for the tables to turn.

I have memories, sensual memories, about things that have never existed. That thin layer of white chocolate on top of the cherry cheesecake. The apple pie with the ginger-sesame crust. The warm, perfectly baked pie that burned in the oven—charred to a crisp and thrown away. They seem innocent enough. But what comes next? Voices from the trees, a heart beating in the palm of my hand, whole rooms convulsing?

My name is Trish and I'm not an alcoholic I'm not even twenty-one yet so I drink sometimes so what who doesn't, it's not like I've been drinking alone and I don't see any of those people here. Okay sometimes I do drink alone why not, who the fuck are you to judge you're not getting me to hold hands with a bunch of losers pumped up on coffee and cigarettes in this crummy New Jersey church basement and recite the Lord's prayer.

That reminds me. I smoked a bunch of my friend Todd's Benson and Hedges 100s last night no wonder my throat is sore now I feel like shit with this hangover and all those stupid dreams I had about seeing my mother who's dead in a diner eating ice cream, only she turned into this disgusting half-naked drag queen with a belly button that poked out like a finger or baby penis and she had all this ghoul makeup on and then I kept driving up and down this hill with some asshole who said he was in love with me, it was like we were in that video game where you steer the car while everything whizzes by and you try to avoid the trucks and shit that appear out of nowhere and when you run into something like a tree the car flips over it's a red convertible and you and your friend sit on the grass dazed for a second then you get back in and go on.

It was like that only we didn't hit anything even though we went faster and faster and I told him to stop giving me this macho showoff shit it wasn't going to make me fall in love with him, take me home I'm not going to fuck you which is just as well because if I did I'd hate you in the morning and this way we can still be friends and I can call you up and say Let's go to that Cuban restaurant in the East Village and eat *ropa vieja* or to the Cambodian one where the waitress is in love with Tab Hunter who she saw on a TV movie and thinks is a young contemporary movie star, she just got here from the farm in Thailand. Welcome to America I said, I didn't say anything about Tab Hunter, let her get the bad news from somebody else. I could call you up to go dancing and you could swing me around and we wouldn't look stupid like those geeks last night at the club where we talked about art and serial killers and about that shithead who wrote me a poison letter because I'd made some comment that was supposed to be supportive but he took it the wrong way the paranoid asshole now there's a real alcoholic for you that guy was pathetic.

It's so hard to remember conversations when everything falls into the black hole of more drinks and twenty trips to the bathroom where the graffiti says "Every poem is a bank account accumulating interest in an existential mutual fund" and "Why am I reduced to this" and the weird woman who does handwriting analysis is in there by the mirror with her stack of raggedy papers and doesn't remember that she once accused my date of touching her ass as we walked by and then tried to get him thrown out what a laugh, who would want to touch her ass maybe the guy on 42nd St. screaming about Jesus with his Pignose amp and dirty suit but nobody else. Random words come dribbling out of the black hole the next day, Clinton Cher O.J. brothers fathers Zen AIDS clothes magazines Gauguin Long Island old boyfriends revolution Moon Zappa Bosnia M & Ms movies parties abortions salud, salud.

Sometimes when I drink I act like a slut. Like the other night I was at this fancy Harper and Row party for somebody's wine guide that just came out not that I knew him or anything, my friend Sam took me but once we'd stuffed our faces with hors-d'ouevres—meat sliced to transparency wrapped around breadsticks and some salmon shit in flowerets on crackers—and drunk a few glasses of wine that a Central American refugee in a tuxedo kept filled, I noticed a guy staring at my blue nail polish and dumped Sam for him. I already explained about not fucking anybody because of the hatred factor but I still feel like a slut making out with guys in elevators and then going home and passing out and waking up in the middle of the night to take Advil and drink water and swear I won't do that again and wonder where my true love is and why my mother had to die on the New Jersey Turnpike two days before my eighteenth birthday which I had to spend at the fucking funeral home and talking to relatives I hate who tried to make me eat crap like potato salad and pot roast.

Last night Todd and I were in this restaurant eating pepper steak and black beans and drinking Dos Equis still relatively sober when a fucked-up old woman came in, she smelled like the bathrooms in Penn Station and looked like all the junkies and losers who hang out there with their scabby hands extended and she had the nerve to ask for a fucking dollar, like why doesn't she pick on Yuppies or somebody with money. We gave her a quarter to get rid of her and then the Puerto Rican woman came by with her crummy roses she probably sells to support her seventeen children and grandchildren so Todd bought a rose and handed it to me and our fingers touched and I pulled them away and today I looked and couldn't find it, it's probably wilted already anyway. Maybe it's in the car wherever I parked it with the congealing remains of the steak that I took the rest of to go, or maybe it's in the street somewhere or being swept up from the floor of the club by the black bald one-armed janitor, anyway the Puerto Rican woman looked creepy like the flower seller in that movie "A Streetcar Named Desire" who walks through saying *Flores para los muertos*, flowers for the dead which is what I'll be before joining AA I just came here to cruise anyway but you people are a drag maybe it's in the bathroom of the club on the back of the toilet I have a distinct image of that in my mind.

Reproduction Synthesis
Mark Tursi

> *Multitude, solitude: terms that, to the active and*
> *fruitful poet, are synonymous and interchangeable. A*
> *man who cannot people his solitude is no less incapable*
> *of being alone in a busy crowd.*
>
> -Charles Baudelaire

She has a run in her stocking, but this does not bother me. Punctuation ended for me long ago. I ignore the run and become mesmerized by the way she smokes her cigarette—long patient inhales that fill her lungs and make the cigarette a part of her. She does not notice I am watching, or pretends not to care. I wish I were being watched.

Perhaps it is improper to speak about sex to a woman enjoying a cigarette so much, but my lust is reaching feverish proportions. If I speak now it might be construed as misogyny. The two are seldom reconciled. The proportion of accidents with words is immense. Punctuation has made clear vision impossible.

She smokes one cigarette after the other and the cloud of smoke around her is a projection. It shields her from the neon of bar lights and perhaps even the mirror behind the bar. My body is coaxing me to action. The shock of this thought keeps me glued to my chair. The fear of crossing the mirror. I am certain that her hands are as cold as indifference. The way one fails to make a choice about leaving.

The smoke does not shield me and I am reminded of how I am looked at, or how my looking thinks I am looked at. The mirror allows me to see all of her: the magenta colored lips that pucker like a tunnel when she inhales. But, even these lose shape, become threadbare, like everything else. One must always expect reproach, restlessness when love is mentioned, even internally.

It is not a she but a they. The crowd is a wave of insomnia talking so fast, incomprehensible. I have not slept.

We will be bumping elbows soon. It is all about where we are and where we are not. The crowd "grows" from a murmur to a din to an insurmountable clamor, even when you are alone. These words make love into a disease, but I am not helpless.

She is really sitting on the porch in front of my house and is someone I care for deeply, alone. It is not stockings after all, but a slight scar. No, it is not really a scar, but the memory of one that happened long ago, perhaps during childhood. You know how it is: sometimes your skin remembers better than you do.

Kitchen on Fire
Ted Pelton

the fire / the guitar / the kitchen / the cowboy hat

I was making an omelette in the kitchen. I was using the guitar to break the eggs. It is very difficult to make omelettes this way, as you know. I don't know how the fire started. I tried to put it out with my guitar. It is easier to put out a fire with a guitar than to break eggs with it such as are fit to use in an omelette, if the fire is small. If a large fire, the guitar is probably more useful with the omelette eggs. In either case, the guitar is unlikely to be of much use as a guitar after being used to put out a fire, as you know. It is likely to no longer be a guitar.

A cowboy hat can put out a fire. I think I have even seen this done on TV, as perhaps have you. And if it is the cowboy hat which is on fire in the kitchen the guitar can be used to put it out, and will be used more profitably in this way than in attempting to break eggs such as may be used in an omelette, as we have seen.

I prefer to play a guitar.

In the kitchen. There's someone in the kitchen, I know. The kitchen in this instance is also a bedroom. This is a famous song on guitar. There is also a banjo, and the banjo is likewise something else as well in the famous guitar song, as we all know. Someone's in the kitchen with a banjo, we know, and someone else is there as well, and the kitchen is not just a kitchen, and the banjo is not just a banjo. And there will be a fire. That's what the singer on guitar is telling us in the famous song, that you can't have a banjo in a kitchen without the potential of starting a fire.

The fire / the guitar / the kitchen / where is the cowboy hat?

The cowboy hat is atop the head of a man in a yellow suit. The yellow suit is sprinkled with large black musical notes. The large musical notes are metonymic, that is, they mean nothing in themselves, not on a staff, with no time signature, but floating in space, the space of the man's yellow suit, suggesting something about the man who wears the cowboy hat and who also has a guitar, that is, establishing in a sense the man's guitar even if we were not to see it. But there it is.

If we were to say, "This is a man who can do anything with a guitar," no one would assume anything to include breaking eggs for an omelette or putting out a fire. One might assume he could start a fire, this man who can do anything with a guitar, but the fire meant would be the type of fire that is also something else, as we know. In fact, this is also suggested by the musical notes, floating on the yellow space of his suit, because only a man who could start a type of fire with his guitar would wear such a suit, which is to say that the notes on the suit are metonyms, as we have already seen, as we all know. So where above we saw that a guitar can be used to put out a fire we all know that in another sense a guitar does not put out a fire, it can only start one. Yet it is also true what is contended in the first sense, that a guitar can't start a fire, not alone, no, it can only be used to put one out, as we all know. There's fire and then there's fire, as we all know.

The cowboy hat / the fire / the guitar / But who is it now that's in the kitchen?

A woman is in the kitchen. Ah, that changes things. Before there was a man and we asked what he was doing but then we saw the guitar or the banjo and we said, "Ah." And the woman, or a woman, was probably there too then, what with the banjo and the kitchen that was not just a kitchen and the fire that was starting, but there was nothing said of a woman before and now there is a woman in the kitchen alone and things have changed. Ah, yes, things have changed. Now she's wearing a cowboy hat. Is it too large? No, it fits her. It is her cowboy hat. Even so, we don't say cowgirl hat. Cowboy hat. It, that is, the hat, contains a space and the space is filled by her perfectly and so we say it fits. And there is no fire. Everything is calm. There is no guitar, no banjo. Quiet. Just a woman in the kitchen with a cowboy hat. Ah, things have changed. The space is filled by her perfectly.

The kitchen / the cowboy hat / Where is the fire?

There is fire within her. She is a fiery woman. There is a fire in her heart. Her nerves are on fire. There is quiet, no guitar, no banjo, but not everything is calm. There is a letter in her hands. She looks at it, keeps looking at it, then looks up. She doesn't know why she's in the kitchen. She catches her reflection in something in the kitchen. A window, the tea kettle, the stainless steel of a spoon. Her reflection upside down. Her nerves on fire. Her reflection wearing a cowboy hat. Why is she wearing a cowboy hat? She doesn't know. There is a fire in her heart. It fits the space perfectly. There is a letter in her hands in the reflection in the window or the kettle or the spoon in the kitchen and her reflection, large or small, fits the space perfectly, even with her head in the cowboy hat. The hat does not put out the fire that is in her heart or that burns her nerves. The fire is in the kitchen but the kitchen is not on fire. It is the letter. The letter discovered left in the cowboy hat from a man who played guitar, but there is not guitar and the guitar started no fire, no, not this fire.

There was an omelette. Made with a guitar? Yes, made with a guitar, each egg cracked with difficulty so as to still be useful in an omelette, and it was silly. Talk of a guitar and of putting out a large fire. How do you put out a large fire? Not with a guitar. Not with a cowboy hat. All silly. How is it she now finds herself in the kitchen? Silly. Her nerves are on fire. She takes off the cowboy hat and puts the letter back inside. It fits the space perfectly.

There was a song. There was someone in the kitchen. There was a banjo. It was a song on guitar. There was a fire. There is a fire in her belly. The kitchen was not just a kitchen, the banjo not just a banjo. Her nerves are on fire. There was a fire started with a banjo. There was a man in a yellow suit with large black musical notes which, if they somehow fell from that space would heap in a pile such as could be set on fire. She remembers the omelette. Everyone always finds themselves in the kitchen and are unsure how exactly they arrived there, as we all know. She discovers a letter left in the cowboy hat. There is a fire in the kitchen.

It's the cowboy hat.

It's the banjo, the musical notes, the guitar, her

nerves.

The fire / The guitar / The cowboy hat.

The kitchen? Someone in the kitchen? Ah, that changes things? Fits the space perfectly?

The yellow space of the suit? The breaking of eggs with a guitar? Fire in the belly?

How do you put out a fire, a very large fire?

How do you put out a fire that fits the space perfectly?

Topographical Models, 1:1
Benjamin Paloff

We had been working on it for years: a full-scale reproduction of everything, combining Borges's map-so-large-that-it-covers-the-world with 3D cities constructed after the fashion of Langweil's paper model of Prague, whose eleven-year creation, detailed down to the very cracks in brick and the arrangement of flowers along those inspiring Hapsburg windowsills, ultimately drained the life of its penniless master in 1837. In our much grander design, painted leaves rattled in the wind, and great fish almost moved through their flammable depths. We marveled at it, challenged each other to find a real stone unrepresented in our schema. We—the obsessive craftsmen, the mayor, the eager youth—had hoped that this would someday demonstrate how we fit into the center of existence, but inevitably we died out. In our ailing city, there were no cemeteries or tombs. To the very last, no one had given any thought to a cure, since no one had believed in disease.

A Pair of Hose Trimmed with Button Eyes, a Lipstick Mouth, Manipulated by So Many Fingers
Christina Milletti

Shiela sat on a table in Examination Room 12, the last in a row of tiny rooms of identical width and depth. Through the paper-thin walls, she could hear other patients shifting their weight on the paper-sheathed tables. Like her, their chins were no doubt curled into their chests. Sheila's table didn't recline. The room was too small: the head-rest was hitting the wall.

Above her, a small fan pulsed. Her paper gown was too short. The room smelled like mothballs and boiled pennies. She wondered how her husband could bear it as he squeezed the tip of his nose through a crack in the door to watch the technician work.

The technician was young. His hands were warm. When he turned one ear toward her ear-like hole, what he heard didn't please him at all.

"How long has this been going on?" he said, his smooth face masking a mild frown.

She grunted. "A week. I didn't know that sound was coming from me."

He nodded. "That's not uncommon. Don't be ashamed." Then he put both of his hands inside her.

Against the doorframe, her husband's voice sounded raspy. "What do you see?" A hinge creaked as he leaned on the door.

The technician ignored him at first. But then Sheila heard an awkward splash and the technician's face brightened at once.

"Hang on."

He leaned forward and, bracing himself, began to pull (she could feel an unwieldy pressure building inside her) and, as the technician drove his weight on her knees, with a yank—a pop and a gurgle—she felt something sudden and large give way.

"That explains it," he said, holding up a shiny trout. Its red belly glowed pink beneath the fluorescent lights. It flapped nervously in his hands.

Sheila propped herself up on her elbows. "Can I touch it?"

The technician shook his head grimly.

"In these cases," he said, "we don't recommend it."

"Does it need water?" Her husband sounded excited as he wriggled his white hands through the door.

"Naturally," the technician said giving it to him. In a moment, her husband was gone.

She was the first to hear the locomotive whistle again—or was it a pile of cars honking in a traffic jam panic?—even though the technician was just a half-step away.

"There's something wrong," she said.

The technician turned at once, listened again at her knees. She could tell he heard it too.

"Hang on."

It's true she found the simple words reassuring. Perhaps it was the way he lilted "hang," then swung firmly to "on" before releasing himself, a boy on a rope, into the narrow cavern of her depths.

This time, when he reached inside her, she could feel his hands grappling past her cervix, unlatching the porthole in her uterine wall, then weaving up through her intestines, his fingers unsnagging knotty reeds before unscrewing her tank and feeling his way out into the rigid cavity of her neck. Onward and upward, he navigated her planet until, his palms cupping her larynx, she feared his hands would pry open her jaws, emerge from her mouth, reach down and over to scratch his own back.

"Ahhhh," he said thoughtfully when she gagged on his pinky. It was as if she had depressed his tongue in order to examine his throat. Not the other way around.

With a determined grin, he was at it again, bracing himself, tugging and reeling—he must have snared a very big fish—until with a relieved sigh, a bit of extra line, he finally relaxed and sat back.

This time, he held a tin can tied to a piece of rope. The line, she could see, led back inside her. Baffled, he merely stared at it at first. But then comprehending (he was a bright, young fellow), he put the tin can to his ear.

She could hear the sound more clearly now. It wasn't a roar or a whistle, but a babbling crowd, a citizenry demanding a word on the line, a room full of complaints.

The technician was nodding and grunting; he seemed to be taking notes. His eyes rolled into the back of his head.

"I hear you," he said, when he put the tin can to his mouth. "Tell me: is there anything else?"

This time the chatter was softer. More subdued. The technician was reassuring. Hadn't she told her husband as much?

"I'll pass the message on at once," he said. Then he set the tin can between her thighs.

"What is it?" Her husband was back at the door. She hadn't seen him return.

She waited. The technician had closed his eyes. He was struggling to recall all that he'd heard. Evidently, he was conscientious too.

He took a deep breath.

"The thermostat," he said, "is set is way too high. The men need shovels. The women hats. The stockyards are out of curry. There are squirrels in every turbine. Your undercarriage has been done in by mice. The pervasive wind smells like cabbage. There were tremors yesterday. A quake today. The ants grow big inside the walls. Your currency is worthless. Army tanks patrol the beach. All the orange thread has disappeared. Tarps are needed. Kerosene. But, most of all, ball peen hammers."

From the hall, she heard her husband curse. But, relieved, Sheila sat back.

"Is that all?" she said, as her head knocked the wall.

The technician shrugged.

"Everyone," he said, "is moving on to another land."

Five postcards from an Athens-bound plane
Nickole Brown

1.

S ister, every day I worry: will I have enough water to swallow that pill? Big as a bee's head and Pepto pink, silly that it could keep you from a baby. But think: jazz, swimmers, cells with water moccasin tails that smell of a pear tree, a suburban blooming, a little nauseating with petals that bruise brown on the ground.

But who wants to carry a baby through security? It's one shoe off, then the other, and the belt too, the underwire and the bobby pins always getting you anyway. He'll yell, *I need a female check!* and off I go into the glass partition, barefoot and wishing I'd worn socks. *Stand on the designated spot, ma'am. Raise your arms palm up, ma'am. Now, I'm going to check you here with the back of my hand. . . .*

Then the Turkish woman with her two babies. Twins, boys. One light, one dark, both crying. *This seat is empty,* I tell her, hoping I can hold one, especially a Turkish one, exotic in his simplicity, tiny denim overalls and white shirt, downy eyebrows already grown into a V down his nose. *Sit here,* I tell her again, romanticizing it all: the mother, Pinar he calls her, stubble on her chin, burying her face into the child's chest while he pulls at her hair. Fierce little hands, wanting.

2.

I pray when the wheels go up, sister. Because nothing but air sustains us then. Break through the gray film to the unimaginable light, the mostly forgotten light, and try not to think of my spider-bitten, aching left knee, the mundane greenbrown of Kentucky below.

10,000 feet. 30,000 feet. Limited beverage service. Moving south. Two hours closer to our dying grandmother. Two hours away from my bird-chested boyfriend, and mama, our mama, clicking around J.C. Penney's Hair Salon with three telephone lines. The empty marble eyes of my cat and the lamb roll of fat wagging my dog's tail. A sky blue bike against the wall, an unfinished painting. I busy myself with island names. Syllables curved like a woman's breast and thigh: Patrai, Athena, Santorini.

3.

Within four hours a sunset, the exploding star of some city below. Sun rising and the shade I refused to close. Next to me, a girl from Alabama, her *O's* round as peaches, gone to the bathroom to brush her teeth in a sink you have to fill to get water from. Will Cindy be waiting, wrinkled pink sweater and a half-smile that says *I told you I would come?*

Sister, this trip is too scheduled for me, one wakeup call after the next, air-conditioned sedans with admissions fees pre-paid, the Acropolis (The Acropolis!) with mouse ears included. I am sick and my left leg never quits aching. The tulip magnolia at home quietly drops her pink panties to the grass. A raccoon walks over the dry garden wondering what things will grow there that he can eat. A sparrow furrows and sleeps under one wing, and in the morning she'll make her way to my window again, tapping her urgent message out on the glass with her black, black beak.

4.

Sister, people are not pretty on planes. A dream of waiting. A lady in black, skin stretched to a powdery flawless white. Cheetah-faced. *I want to say I know, I can tell. You were beautiful once.*

When I called home yesterday, mama answered the phone with an exhausted *yes*. *Stop calling me,* she didn't say. *Just have a good time.* Not like Aunt Tony though, no. *If you were mine,* she said. *If you were mine, you wouldn't go. But you ain't mine. You got to do what your mother tells you to do, because you belong to her.* I belong to mama, mama belongs to a mama that won't be here for long. Then who will she belong to? Me? Can I reverse those charges? Greece: trivial. Family: important. Permanent. Stay. Go. Stay. Go. *Your mama loves you and Hope loves you and your daddy loves you and you need to go. We all think you should go.* A sky blue bike against the wall, an unfinished painting.

5.

Grandmother is trying to sleep now too. Dehydrated, she dreams of confetti and Elvis and the hammer they buried with her husband. She is not dreaming of diarrhea stains, the broken footboard of her bed held together with picture wire, the nicotine glaze of a chandelier hanging crooked over the kitchen table. A cereal bowl is full of her hair rollers and years of nerve pills, saved for what I don't know. Her skin is smooth and thin as a Bible page.

What's under that white smog? I'll know, quick as it takes you to watch a sitcom. Feast on your life, sister. Feast.

Mother: "I almost eloped once. When I was seventeen."

What happened?

Mother: "I got a very bad stomach ache and he left without me."

In the newspapers someone is always searching the ocean for a black box. A record of what was said by the pilots before the crash. The search for a black box can go on for weeks after the search for survivors has ended. If the cause of the crash can be determined, the public will be reassured that similar accidents may be prevented in the future.

Aunt: "She was still a teenager when she met your father. He waited four years to marry her. Supposedly, your father stopped in to see his mother after the first time he saw her and said, 'I just met the girl I'm going to marry.'"

On the radio the announcers are always careful to say, "the so-called black box, or cockpit voice recorder, was recovered." So-called. One announcer explains that the black box, "was located by the" (she pauses) "'pinging' sounds it emits."

Uncle: "Your mother had a hard time in high school. She had a nervous breakdown and dropped out and moved to a commune in Vermont."

One transcript from a cockpit voice recorder includes the voice of an aircraft maintenance engineer speaking to the pilots over the radio. He refused to believe what they were telling him. Damage to the plane had resulted in the loss of all hydraulic systems. The pilots could no longer steer the airplane. The engineer thought this was very unlikely, even impossible. He asked the pilots to verify their loss six times before the plane crashed.

Mother: "The man who did it was an old family friend. He had helped my sister find a job. My parents didn't say anything when I told them. They acted as if nothing had happened. They still invited him over to dinner and let my sister go over there to work in his darkroom. That's when I left home."

My mother has three daughters, but she only told this story to her son.

The black boxes are not black, they are bright orange.

Aunt: "She got her GED in Vermont. Then she went to California for a few years and lived with Liz and Bernie. She worked in a sandwich shop or a Chinese restaurant, I think. One day she just got tired of it and called up Roger to tell him she was ready to marry him. That was it. He came and got her."

She once hitchhiked across the country with truck drivers because she missed her bus in Chicago. She had not needed anyone to come and get her then. Maybe she just got tired of living a life with an unrecognizable shape.

Mother: "Your father taught me how to drive. I had never driven a car before we were married. Our first apartment had a driveway with cement walls. I would scrape the car against the walls almost every time I parked it and I had worn all the paint off one side of the car. Roger and his brother spent a whole weekend sanding it down and repainting it. The day after his brother went back to Syracuse, I scraped it against the wall while I was parking and ruined the new paint job."

My sister admits that she is terrified of making the same mistakes our mother made.

Mother (to herself, from inside her room): "I ruin everything."

I admit to my sister that I don't want to let anyone take care of me.

Grandmother: "Roger must have put her through college. I don't know how he did it, he was still in medical school then. I don't know where she got the money. She never asked us for a dime."

My mother's education includes hours of anatomical drawing of birds from life, the study of fine woodworking and cabinet making with a German master, and a bachelor's degree in English.

Mother: "I couldn't stand his friends from medical school. They were all pompous and awkward. They knew how to memorize but they didn't know how to be human. Rochester was cold and ugly. Everything there was the same color. I was incredibly lonely."

She had her first child that year.

Malcolm McPherson recently collected a book of transcripts from cockpit voice recorders called, The Black Box: All-New Cockpit Voice Recorder Accounts of In-Flight Accidents. *It is the updated version of a 1984 "classic." On some of these flights, there were no survivors. Only voices were salvaged.*

Mother: "If your father got his residency in Iowa I would have gone to graduate school there. I was already accepted. He was sent to North Carolina instead."

The transcripts in Malcolm McPherson's book were edited by the National Transportation Safety Board before he published them. Any emotional material was deleted. The curses and apologies that were yelled out just before the crash were deleted. Only material useful to the public in determining the cause of the crash remained.

Mother: "I'm amazed that more people don't commit suicide. They just keep on living. It's so hard and they just keep doing it."

Useful to the public?

Mother: "Whenever I told him I wanted to work he would tell me that it didn't make any sense. He would say, 'there's no reason for you to work if you'll never be able to make even a fraction of what I make.'"

She hit her thumb with the hammer over and over, nailing wood paneling onto the ceiling of the shed to make a place for me to write. She wanted me to take myself seriously as an artist. Her thumbnail fell off.

All the pilots whose voices are recorded in The Black Box *had extensive training and experience, but many were reluctant to actually fly their planes themselves. The use of autopilot contributed to several crashes. In at least one crash, which resulted in the death of 279 people, the crew might have saved the plane even in the final seconds if they had, "flown the airplane with their own hands."*

Mother: "Rumi wrote that...roughly...the only thing that will be with you to your grave is your work. Only your work will speak for you after you're gone."

There are photographs, as evidence. In every photograph she wears the same strange expression. It's a look I've seen on zoo animals. She had dreams about panthers in cages.

Uncle: "I remember when she visited back then she was like a person living under water. She wandered around with you in a basket on her back like a zombie."

There are only two photos where she seems to be really smiling. Her wedding picture and the formal portrait of her with me, her first child.

Mother: "He used to say that you could lock me in a closet and I'd still get something out of it. I guess that's true."

An investigation of a crash usually also includes the recovery and intensive examination of any debris.

Mother: "I could never keep the house clean. I don't know why."

My sister and I tried to make candles and spilled the hot wax all over the linoleum floor. Our baby brother vomited on the rug.

Aunt: "The place was such a wreck. Your mother was so overwhelmed, she just couldn't keep it clean. You had written all over the walls and burned the table by the time you were two. There were toys everywhere, clothes, dirty dishes in the middle of the floor."

She spent a lot of time in the garden.

Mother: "I felt very… empty."

She also wrote poetry.

Mother: "I did nothing but take care of babies for ten years. Each time one of you stopped being a baby I had another one. I feel like I never got the chance to enjoy any of you as children."

On one of the first days of spring she told me to go outside and lie face down in the clover.

Mother: "I hate to think that there was something I could have done or some kind of drug I could have taken. After spending so much of my life depressed, I hate to think that it didn't have to be that way."

My conversations with my mother consist mostly of silence.

Mother: "………………………………………….."

There is no way of knowing exactly what the pilots are doing during the silences on the recordings. Reading their instruments? Manipulating the controls? Looking out the window?

Mother (over and over again): "What you have to understand about men is that they aren't like us. They don't have feelings."

My father talks more than my mother, and more easily. But he rarely talks about her.

Father: "One of the things I miss about your mother is the poetry she brought into my life. I still keep a copy of Rumi in the drawer of my desk."

One line of one transcript must have been overlooked by the National Transportation Safety Board. As the plane was going down the pilot said, "Help me hold it. Help me hold it. Help me hold it." The other pilot yelled, "Amy, I love you!"

Mother: "When I started working as a sculptor he told me I was wasting my education. He said, 'I didn't pay for your degree so that you could go off and play with clay.'"

She talks to herself as she hollows out a stoneware bowl. She is saying something about containment. She talks to her dogs and to the chickens. She has said so many things that have gone unheard. Off the record.

Mother: "He made me feel like I wasn't really a writer if I wasn't published. It was as if my poetry didn't mean anything unless it was accepted by someone else."

After the divorce she started her own literary magazine with another woman. She also became a dancer.

One pilot sang a lullaby as his plane went down.

Mother (In an interview for the position of choreographer. She had no experience.): "I have life experience."

On certain evenings in dark motels, she could transform her lip into the edge of the bottle, imagining her face was made of amber glass and the men paused above her only to take a drink of breath. Over the years, men drank and drank until there were only two sips left inside. They began sucking the air out of the glass that grew warm in the wrong places because of heat radiating off their hands. The men's breath along with white feathers fell over autumn winds drifting through open windows. As the chill receded, hands and dry leaves glided over shadows mingling and flitting above. Girls woke to conformed arrangements of bottlenecks, brittle stems of wineglasses shattered on the balcony stairs. Witness to her own departure in hazy mirrors, she would seek herself in other women, their singsong voices echoing through chimneys of the houses she had left behind, fingers tracing the rails of the locked stairwell. Recalling the perfume drifting through dark halls, the way scent caught in curtains along with silence, she found more intricacy and misconceptions in common things— bottles, hands, and leaves—than in labyrinths designed for deliberate confusion, as in a crowded subway, passages leading onto passages. Leaves became refuse in the winter, raked into piles for burning. In the heat of flames, one could drink from a cold bottle and still be thirsty. Looking at the leaves, one could spit whiskey into the fire and watch it flare, turning old magazines and newspapers into black feathers lost on the wind. Like a fortuneteller, one could rub coal into the creases of a woman's hands to tell her age during the years when she was still alive. Shuffling through black and white photographs littered with occasional sepia tones like ash on broken glass, women feared her, saying she was a man because she loved them so.

But
Kim Addonizio

They'd known each other a month and had decided to marry, but two days before the wedding she hit him over the head with a beer bottle during an argument and the paramedics had to come and he got sixteen stitches but what the hell, they reconciled as soon as they were sober. And then the wedding, a party in the warehouse space he lived in, and everyone still drinking and dancing as they headed off to a big hotel in the city. But the friend who was going to loan them a Lincoln to arrive in style never showed up, so they took the groom's old car and pulled up and staggered into the lobby, but with his bandaged head and the two of them being pretty wasted and some kind of complication about the name on the credit card--another friend had arranged for the room—the hotel refused to let them register. So back to his car, the old car that had no passenger window and now wouldn't start. He tried to hotwire it but somehow pulled out the ignition wire instead, after a while he got the car going but it had started to rain, hard, and they had to drive back home with her getting soaked and him holding one hand out the window to help the wiper blade sweep back and forth. At home the party was still going but by now the two of them wanted to be alone, and a nasty argument broke out between the groom and a few revelers who didn't want to leave, but finally they did and the newlyweds went to sleep after the bride threw up in a hand-painted ceramic pasta bowl someone had given them. In the morning they made love and things seemed better but when she got out of bed to pee she stepped on a piece of glass from a broken bottle, maybe the one she'd broken over his head the other night or maybe one of the several that had been broken the night before, and it was back to calling the ambulance and now no one has seen them for three days but they're probably fine, just holed up together in marital bliss, not killing each other with one of the guns he keeps, sometimes things start out badly but get better, by now they're surely better, they couldn't possibly screw things up any further but maybe they could.

The dream stood aside and told me that it would be called "the dispirited, small ditch," and taught me to stand aside as well. I said I would be a reporter and gather news even though I knew in secret that I had been a witness. Therefore, I stood literally to the side of the door while someone else asked the grieving mother for the story of her son. How darkening skin makes for sleep, and he slept. And I knew that my own brother and son had cried at this, a fact. He made his own loss out of what happened at night, the indentation in the road where sleeping people go. Then, at the lit white doorway, the mother turned from the reporter and called me a witness, and seemed to forgive me for it. All that I admitted. The "V" gesture I made to signify ditch or collision.

Elevation
Nina Shope

SANTA FE

M.,

The colors here seem too vivid now. The bright orange rooms, in which Mexican lamps hang plentiful as stars, are almost blinding to me. And the chili peppers are like tongues rooted and torn. Strung translucent. I find myself filling our room with mirrors—hung in careful patterns across the walls or spread out on the floors, in hope of catching some trace of you. But instead I see myself reflected from too many angles. And again, it is blinding.
—N.

M.,

In our room, the ristras have rotted. The moths have infested them all. Attracted to the wreaths as if they are filled with a light we cannot see. Or maybe you can. I cracked one open yesterday to find it filled with larva—thick webbing, their wormlike bodies. I hope they are nowhere near you.
—N.

M.,

I am afraid that, without you, I cannot survive this city. And wonder whether I should return to New York. What stops me, I think, is that they petition their dead here, like I do. In New York, I would have to resign you to the ground. Here they live with the saints intimately. And the dead still have days to visit.
—N.

M.,

Last night I placed a pepper on my tongue to absorb the taste. But I am frightened to remove it. It seems to have become a second organ of speech, filling my mouth with fire.
—N.

M.,
I leave peppers on the pillows. Fill the room with them. Drying them on doorknobs, over the bed, on the windows. I place them in my mouth. Press them between my thighs. It feels as if I am trying to burn something out of me.
—N.

M.,
Some type of resurrection. When caught in the mirrors, I freeze solid. I sleep for days. Today I awake surrounded by tongues. Speaking in tongues. Solitary. Surrounded by mirrors. I awake translucent. Burning. I awake to lanterns circling me like half open eyes. I awake during the festival of lights. I awake on the Day of the Dead. I awake with my tongue torn at the root.
—N.

NEW YORK

M.,
I am careful to only eat bland foods now—rice and yogurt, small perforated crackers wiped free of salt. I walk quickly past the rows of Indian restaurants on 6th street. They seem to house implosions of light and color—each one strung wall to wall with Christmas lights, stranded with glitter, with mirrored balls and sequins. I saw one today which had plastic chili lights hanging down in fleshy strands that made the entire room look like an aorta. And I knew I had to turn away. That placed upon my tongue, the pepper would fill me with blazing electrified light. With a current too intense to control. And everything now must be about control.

My mother told me months ago that this runs in my family – my grandfather and his brother. One of them never made it out of the hospital, and the other in and out for shock treatments and lithium. It made me think more about my father, roaming the house ranting to himself, his scarlet face and clenched teeth. My mother never connects him to this lineage – when I question her, she says that he is only thinking aloud. She says, "you know philosophers."

169

But, by "know," she means "understand." And that is one thing I cannot do.
—N.

M.,
When I walk through the subway here, I must be careful to avoid the men's spit. It sickens me, the way they insist on sharing even this moist inner part of themselves, such a public physicality. I try to leave as little trace of myself as possible—Lysoling the computer keyboard after I have used it, walking so lightly that I do not leave footprints or a single smudge of dirt behind me. I know there is something urgent in this. I do not want to create a trail—anything that could be followed.
—N.

M.,
I have realized that what is necessary to convince my parents that I am sane is stillness. I must learn to move my hands less and cross my legs more and above all, not to speak. When they talk to me, their language changes. Word by word, the adjectives drop out of their vocabularies. They only use nouns and verbs, words meant to convey solidity, simplicity, a sense of order.

I know that it is important to avoid questions. I remember this. Something about a family history with the fragments missing. That I must not ask about the day my grandmother walked into a room to find both her brothers dead. Must not ask about my great aunt whose son met a similar end, muscles atrophied in the wheelchair, or about my grandmother's guilt for having son after healthy son. My grandmother once told me there was a curse upon this family. That my parents had prayed for daughters. I remember spending nights wondering why my body did not succumb to this wasting disease. Something about boys and the way they are born.

I know now that this is why I loved you. The strange contours of your body. The way your spine twisted. The weak and frail bones of your legs. How, when I would wrap around you at night, our bodies were as entangled as the

ristra hanging from the window ledge. Do you remember my ridiculous theory that the heat of the city would relax your muscles, that your body would unwind in the harsh New Mexican sunlight? I am ashamed to say that I am not sure I would have loved you like that—straightened out entirely. I think something inside me must be twisted—wasn't that something you often said? You made it sound like a compliment, like something you admired. I am not sure you should have. I am unsure of many things.
—N.

M,
Do you think it was strange that even though we were both Jewish, we would walk into churches and rub ourselves with dirt that was supposed to heal believers? The crutches hanging like crosses on the walls. I remember sitting underneath the santuario's famous staircase, the perfect double helix that curved like a spine twisting supinely. We said this place would heal us both. Even when we knew it would not.
—N.

M.,
I think how hard it must have been for my parents to fly down and get me – to open the door and find a room filled with the raw earthiness of rotting peppers, filled with moths. Their daughter surrounded by mirrors, unable to speak, tongue seared by chili. My mother cannot understand it, having prayed so hard to avoid having sons, only for her daughter to cling instantly to a boy she had to know would die. And I must have, mustn't I? I imagine she was desperate to get me away from that city, where they worship too heavily the cult of broken male bodies. Angered by the crucifix affixed to our wall. Of course, it is something we never talk about.
—N.

M.,
When I came down from that altitude, my lungs contracted as if all the air had left them. I have learned to breathe shallowly in this city, with its utter lack of elevation. It is

unnatural how easily the air enters here. And I do not want it in me.
—N.

M.,
I do not tell anyone, but I remember everything about that place. How we hung a tin lamp, cut in the shape of a star, above the bed. Our Polaris—its tarnished constancy. The brittle streams of light that broke from its body like a nova. The tiers of lanterns left on the stairs at night.

I remember backbones sold in a bowl at the flea market. Scraped out so that we could still see where the marrow used to be. The woman behind the booth putting a string through them and pulling suddenly—a whole spine recreated right before us. I remember books of martyrs and the way we bent over them late at night. Shrines with Christ leaning heavily into his nails, like a mourner relying on hands to keep him from falling. And the staircase at the santuario—wondering what it would be like to curve and curve and not break. I remember how the clouds hung like bodies over the mountains. The hour at which the adobe took on the color of coagulation and injury. Until it made you feel ill and you refused to look at yourself in any mirror.

It was unbearable how quickly the moths settled in afterwards. And the larva. Attracted to the red centers of the peppers. I drank water at first, to keep them away from me. Scared that the dryness, the rawness, would draw them to me. But it burned when I swallowed and everything felt hollow. Unable to catch an angle of you anywhere. Chilies twisted to resemble your body. Until that was the only thing I wanted. The slow incineration. The emptiness. Larva filling the peppers. Placed on my tongue, they were the only trace of you. Blistering. Speechless. And the moths flew closer then, as if I'd drawn the light into me. When I left the city, I thought that might be the way you would find me. Lit up from the inside like a lantern. I would have traded even speech for that—the ability to draw you to me.
—N.

M.,

I sleep in a room with sky blue sheets and think of the nights when we would lie in the shape of the northern cross, polaris above us—cautiously luminous. I have tried to take that radiance into me, but even it is fading. And in this room there are no directionals. Nothing to navigate by. Across the water, I can see the bridge illuminated like a string of lanterns or blue beads, too fragile to touch, let alone to stand upon. Tankards slung so low in the water that they give the impression of perpetually sinking. Half-submerged. The lights of the city like stars failing. I try to go to sleep remembering the clustered constellation of your sex. That dark space on the bed that I moved towards again and again. Until the lights drop into the water like fireflies dying on lawns in late August. The blue of the water and the bed always invades my sleep at night. Trying to extinguish the mirrors spread out like moons, the dreams from which I awake dry and strung out as a ristra. Suspended.

—N.

Pilgrim
Ed Taylor

(on the street in washington, dc)

Walking 15th with my blindfold tight & treasury head's no help with directions, will not answer my scream. i do tend to wander in the mind. my family says i'm not right in the head: then i should be left alone— get it? i say, but they never do.

which way to go? why not i as king bee or turtle dove, blake engraving, page on fire, anything but a white hair on god's black bustier; beg a little something for the pain—limbs ache from swinging at the low curves of more doubts than you can shake a bible at. which way to vote? thumbs up or down, on derry, on gaza, on comet, on vixen. i pluck a piece of 3rd avenue el out of my scalp & wing it at all maos, jesuses & e. e. cummings-es.

which way to live? while angels meringue on some pin's head i wade out to wait for the light, & bob & bing now swing my way, got up in blue. they help me off the sawhorse I copped & say, don't block the limos of justice.

my ride ends in their eyes: petition for asylum denied.

so hell they lead me to shore & grin & now i must begin again. the sawhorse stays hungry & alone.

The bird-like lights are hovering over Albuquerque where there is the easy living of Quonset hut casinos and the flashing blue circle of the Creamland sign near the abandoned transfer station.

Walking around the rim of his home, a 180-degree house, half the circumference of the volcano's vista, he says, if his life is a geological form, my father wishes for a place to step on all the edges of each red mesa and plateau where the rich dirt has piled up, he says

if I could thread these sides together
I would have a 360-degree home
a crater without seams, a center of *success*. Success lies in the layers of dirt, each one took hundreds upon hundreds of years to build up. If I dig here, I might find a flint-carved arrowhead that gleams at all of its edges, a place to build an underground room that is warm in the winter, cool in summer, and I could sweep the dirt off the floor right into the river.

Instead, I had $10 to get out of _____ de Navidad, tearing the door off its hinges in Teotihuacán and getting thrown in jail, mediocre out-of-body experiences ripping into muscle and pitching me against the wall. I've chickened out on all my visions—in my current state, I now have this clarity of mind—they were just bad pharmaceutical speed.

If there were a home to go home to, I'd go to San Ignacio, Widow's Tears (so-called because that stream dried up so fast each year); I'd get an extension on the story of my former life with creeks.

Red taillights slipping across the mesa, mountains rising out of the plain, winterfat bushes like chubby white wicks scrubbing up the dirt. Everybody wants to get home this Sunday night, greasy weekend feeling inside.

Is it my brother or is it my boyfriend or is it my father or my misbehaved baby driving across the scene?

Car taking off down 285, roaring like a jet.

A landscape so empty from certain angles that you yourself might feel totally emptied out, guts stored somewhere in the basement of some great desert palace in canopic jars.

Burnt as the piñon stumps out on the scrubland.

Because with nerves as jumpy as mine, ears as acute, world rolling like steam over my eyeballs, on which everything seems to stick — it's better to empty it all out.

Traffic lights ballooning out of the dark, opening like parachutes about to float off the face of the earth.

White houses sailing across brown, blind plains.

Towns in the distance out on the dark solid earth that look like some alien ship came down out of the sky to set up shop; then years later they abandon their little town — they let the humans move in, and the humans said, Let's call this Alamosa, Ft. Garland, Pueblo, Abiqui.

(Think up something new to say about stars.)
The stars look like they're about to pass out.
Pass out, and on to another plane.
(Has somebody already said that?)

We make enough plastic wrap in America each year to shrink wrap the state of Texas. Say something about that and stars.

Tenebrific stars, believed to cause night.

Jon says, I'll say:
I guess the sun's going down in its right place.
    Or:
The sun's going down five inches off tonight — missed its
proper spot — a little drunk I guess! drunk sun!

Truth lies in the mind.
The eye brought it there and buried it, what it saw.

Small angers we hold transparent to reason like pieces of
sharp-edged ice that never melt but float in the body, travel
through lungs and liver and kidneys, settle about the heart,
blind augers; that's history. Shards nearly as polished as
beach glass over time, but wicked enough to rip open a vein
now and again. What are they? What formed them? The
night your mother screamed at your father and you heard
all the words, how your father shook your hand when you
returned from ten months in Europe. What angers and
deceits, what disappointments and rages, weaknesses, let
in the small latches that would later make the whole thing
unhinge?

What is the moral framework of this piece?
Piece of what?
Writing? Life?

The moral is not forgive and forget (though in this story
neither is a moral lapse). The moral is the story, and the
story is a life. The life said

The Invention of Where
Thom Ward

How do you keep the four guys who hate you away from the five who are undecided? Isn't not to be chosen still a choice? What's forgiveness without oblivion? Were incompetence a crime, wouldn't everyone be convicts? And where would we put them? Is there a place dreams meander to dream? Now that we know beauty is merciless, what good is it? When old Spot leaves his spots all over the couch, the recliner, the rug, where, besides the vet, will he go? Isn't heaven just another name for Special Ed.? How do you respond to the white-gloved proctologist? If I fall in the woods and finally stop talking, could anyone else get a word in edgewise? Aren't most of these hours just stand-up tragedy? What's the purpose of ice and Triple Sec without a blender? Even if I was lucky enough to concoct an original thought, where would I put it?

She was a milk-warm girl in bad odor with herself, glad to have at last come down in the world. So she undoubled herself from the boyfriends, the girlfriends, to better herself under my roof. Mornings, she would struggle to the kitchen faucet and put a finger to the underside of the spout. There was usually enough water still hanging from it for the finger to come away with a big, rudimentary drop. This she would use to loosen the crumbles of sleep from the corners of her eyes. Breakfast was just soda she stirred bubbleless with a paper straw.

I was the one stuck making the bed. I'd interrupt myself only long enough to raise a fingertip of her silverous lipstick from the tube, then with rushed reverse turnings send it down again.

Afternoons, the sky volunteered its birds and its sunshowers. We would be out on the patio again, each with a rubble of white chocolate in a ruffled paper baking cup. The one skymark was a radio tower, laddery and ablink.

Anything, she kept demanding, is the seat of a passion.

I would have to remind her, counteringly, that you don't pick the person who fronts your life—you get picked, you watch the picker's ankles vanish into the scrunched socks afterward (his whole body going blank behind the blue-black of the uniform), and the picker goes off in the starkest of transportations: you keep an ear cocked ever after for the return of his van and its paraphernalian clatter in the gravelled driveway.

You might consider chumming away at somebody your own age, she would say. Or who's hailing now from whom?

I would answer that we come by our austere perversions and then do our best to get out from under ourselves.

She wore her T-shirts in wearied, vanishing colors and would hold my hand retardedly in public. A shortstreeted city was a habitual drive away. We would arrive just in time for the waning daytime plenty along the one horizonal avenue. We would walk around the people. The local public! They all had the look of having been made too much of already—each citizen a subsided mystery with hard feelings and staying power.

Afterward, restored to the house, close-piled on veers of the sectional sofa, we would haze each other into a shared, mutual nap. Her lips contributed little to mine, but there were always fresh runs of emotion inside.

Her heart never once cracked down.

Apples the Eat Boy
Brian Clements

On their expedition into the wild of the Congo, they took a boy from his mother to give to the harbor master's wife. The boy grew to be a fine sailor, but he would catch no fish. He would eat only apples and drink only river water. They took him to Church, but he would only sit or stand silently. They did not force him. When the boy turned twelve years old, he disappeared once for twelve days and nights. When he returned he would only say that he needed rest. He carried with him a sack full of deep red apples that grew only over the far ridge.

That June, the harbor master's wife came across a gathering. The boy stood before a small crowd. He said, eat your bread. It is the white of my apple. Drink your wine. It is the skin. They ate their bread and drank their wine. They stole his apples and ate them, too. Then they turned to the boy. But before she could call for help, they had pulled him down and devoured him entirely. Three days later, he appeared at the end of the wharf, handing out apples the shape of hands, which, once bitten, the fishermen discovered too late, throttled the eater.

Where His Mother Paints
Cris Mazza

lectric heaters, one in every room, metal coils glowing silently red, sometimes buzzing, a thin hum, and he decided to pee into his. It spit and hissed, smoked, choked. He stood there aiming, up and down both red coils. And the smell: burning hair, melting plastic, smoldering wool clothes, cooking bugs. There was no smoke. Dad broke the connection so the heater couldn't be turned on. It still stunk. Dad ripped the unit out of the wall. The hole stunk. He got used to it. Dad said he had to. Before the pee

the room smelled of socks, of school lunches hidden and rotting in the closet, of plastic toys, of fishing equipment, frogs and algae. The walls had been painted: green. Even greener cabinets and drawers. Red and blue cowboys and Indians fought wars on the curtains. Sick gray rug (did it used to be another color?). The green drawers were chipped and scuffed from being pulled out and stepped on so he could reach the cupboards or into the fish tank which once tipped over — he shrieked, and the fish lay dancing on the soaked, matted rug. The heater hole

was taped over with cardboard and covered with a green burlap bulletin board — too low, but he could reach without standing on anything. The beds were bunked to allow whole cities to be laid out on the sand-filled rug, or a Lincoln Log fort, or a Tinker-Toy factory, or a Monopoly game that all the stuffed animals played with him for weeks. An old Chinese-red desk for his homework replaced the bulletin board over the heater hole, brought out the red of the Indians in the curtains. The paint on the green walls came off everywhere he taped a poster: Rolling Stones, Santana, Trout of the Western Hemisphere. The aquarium

was drained a final time, a deck and hot tub built just outside the glass doors which had replaced the cowboy and Indian

182

window, the rug ripped out, hardwood floor underneath sanded and polished. After he went away to college. Came back once and slept on the ruffled daybed which had replaced the bunks. The walls were papered, white and muted yellow, the desk moved, painted white, the heater hole patched a final time with white ceramic tile bordered with blue and red patterns, too small to be anything. Mom moved her watercolor things in there, cleaned out the closet, looking for one last petrified sandwich.

The Lightbulb
Martha Ronk

We were sitting on the edge of two twin beds crammed into a tiny road front room. There was an overhead bulb. He sat on one wooden foot of a bed and I on the one next to it as we talked about our lives and what had happened since we had seen each other. Cars went by on the wet street below us.

Years later I was driving along the same street with a friend who asked why I put up with him. I started the story of having met him when he was the best friend of my high school boyfriend who has since died, of having tried, after that moment on the bedsteads, to live with him; and it all seemed as I spoke, as so much does these latter days, irrelevant. It was an account, but the account didn't matter, didn't explain. What seemed relevant, although I have no way of explaining this to myself, were the bedsteads and the particular way in which light from a single bulb made the evening simultaneously etched and lost in a kind of washed melancholy which depends, I am certain, not on the play of memory, although one is tempted to that conclusion, but simply on the light from the lightbulb itself. It was, I thought then and I think now (and not because of the reasons one might find in a story) the causal principle for all that followed.

We sat for a long time in that room getting through stories of our failed marriages, and of our children, all of them still at that moment in time, young and fair and about to be dragged, by us, to the Cape for a summer of sun and sand. My son saw a skeleton in the closet there in his room under the dormers which to this day he remembers as if blaming me for something unforgivable.

She said, driving me to his place, not the apartment with the bedsteads and the lightbulb, but to his house some twenty years later, why do you put up with him. She too possesses a character of great certainty, but of an entirely different sort, certain that we should be kind to one another, gentle in our responses, humble and considerate, and since I agree with her, I am uncertain how to convey my sense that it isn't what's called for, that I can't understand (although clearly I do understand in some way) her question nor frame a response. I think of a story which I don't tell.

What does it mean to put up with anyone, with oneself even. How can understanding, whatever that is, be based on the quality of light in a bedroom of an apartment he took after his wife left him to run off to live to this day in Italy and the sun. He tells the story over and over. We sit in his garden, now twenty years later, and he tells the story, not exactly as if it had just happened, but as the single most important event of his life, although both of us know it is not exactly that, although as story it may be. And so, if I say that my husband had an affair with his wife and that when we tried to throw in our lots together that summer on the Cape after sitting all night in a room with the light from a bare lightbulb, it follows that it was doomed to fail. My son came out of the bedroom into the summer sun frightened of the skeleton in the closet and he saw in my child's face the face of the man who had slept with his wife, a fact which might not have mattered so profoundly if his wife had not later left him and run off , but which, given that event and my son's hallucination and fear, mattered enough to change everything that followed.

At least we changed at that moment in which he saw a man in a child's face, changed, as we had to towards one another and I moved away, he bought a large house with a garden and each of us went on to other times and other people who didn't know the stories, or if they did, because we told them, didn't make much of them except as stories. Nor can I really make much more of it all, except to recognize in the story the importance of the elements which imprint themselves on those who live through them rather than hear them recited. Except the slant of light as it came in through the room as my son came out from under the slanted roof to tell the story of the skeleton in his closet. Except as the imprint of light during the telling becomes part of the way stories are passed on from person to person so that while I was in the car with her twenty years later and trying to think of what it meant "to put up with anyone," I was aware of the overcast sky, a sky so unlike the California one I usually live under, that it became part for me of the telling of the story of how his wife had had an affair with my husband and left us, the man and I, forever locked together in a way that isn't "putting up with," but one's life. That the sympathy one feels is, and here of course one is selfish, for oneself, and not only the person one was when young. It isn't, I wanted to explain to her in the car, that you see him as arrogant, or that he is, but rather that I am, I must be or else I forget all the stories of all that has happened and that is far worse than, in an entirely different category from, dominating the conversation.

And since my husband has disappeared, he is also the link to days he has no exact knowledge of, which I may or may not have told him about, but which had to belong to someone other than me and there are, as I said to him in the garden of the house, so few of us left. Few of us, that is, for whom these particular memories matter so much, imprint themselves so fiercely, so that although he wasn't there on the day I learned to make a dramatic mess of things, to throw dishes across the kitchen against the wall, to break the plaster and ruin the dinner and raise my voice so loud the neighbors came down from upstairs in their longjohns and laughed and my husband laughed and the old flowered dishes we had found in the closet lay in pieces across the floor, he seems to have participated. And because soon my husband, who needed far more drama than the breaking of dishes or even the making up that followed, would have an affair with his wife and would leave the man standing some years later staring at the face of my son in disbelief that he could look so like the father, if that's what it's called when each of us fails the other out of following a story into a life.

And of course, one keeps trying to get back into that room with the lightbulb, not only because one wishes, as all human beings wish, to turn back the clock, have a chance to do it over again, nor because we think that we might work it all out better, but because we wish to see again. Knowing as one knows that we have all changed through time, we wonder what it was like to be in that room with the exact light from the lightbulb and to listen to oneself say things about the way the marriage failed because I could not learn to speak in ways so foreign to my own, couldn't pick up the drama or extend the range of my voice often or far enough. He told me about how lost he felt, like wandering through mazes underground in the dark he said, without purpose or anchor or children. She had taken the children and we were sitting that evening under the lightbulb on the two beds he had bought for his children if they returned, if she agreed to send them for the summer, if she would get them on the plane from Italy to the United States to this room which seemed once I had heard the story, emptier than before, desolate even, so that the quality of the light changed from being the sort of light I might have imagined for a setting in a café where we might have been sitting over watery beer telling our stories for the camera, to a children's bedroom without the children in a certain unforgettable cast of light.

Poems from *Real*
Stephen Ratcliffe

4.30

Dip at the top of the ridge filled by small
white cloud just before the sun first appears,
light grey of sky suddenly brightening above it.
Man in a green shirt dreaming of paddling below
huge breaking wave, shaved-headed man dropping
straight down face. The blond woman thinking
woman who wakes up in the middle of the night
thinking of the man is probably contemplating
exchange of bodily fluids, time to open the door
and turn up the music. Woman in the green chair
seeing that for Heidegger being and becoming are
the same, "bestowing on every presencing a light
in which something present can appear." Silver
of sun's reflection on the water the moment it
finally rises, line of six cormorants lifting
above blinding shoulder of the wave breaking
below it.

5.7

Pale white of full moon hanging behind branches
of acacia in lower left vertical pane of window
above the yellow and blue bed, light grey light
coming into sky above ridge in opposite window.
Woman in blue jeans above man in green shorts
who wants to rip his clothes off to show him
what "mutual" means, man wanting her to listen
to the music on the inside as well as the radio.
Older man hoping there will be wheelchair access
to his sexual peak, the woman spelling a message
in small silver box composed of yellow and blue
and pink letters. Heidegger speaking of Greek
phrase for sink into the clouds, man in black
sweatshirt drawing a box around "entire calm
grey sky." White line of water on the blue
horizon breaking across reef on right, red
orange beak of the tern crossing overhead.

5.8

Parallel lines of window frame's shadow slanting
diagonally across a patch of light cast by small
white circle of moon across the wall to the left
of the unmade yellow and blue bed, moonlit body
of ridge floating in opposite window. The man
looking at close-up of a gold band on woman's
left finger, pair of black shoes beside a pair
of black sandals at bottom of stairwell. Blond
woman with shampoo in her hair who answers phone
in the bath, asking to call the man back in five
minutes. Heidegger thinking Heraclitus is lucid
rather than obscure, who writes of a "lighting
whose shining he attempts to call forth into
language of thinking." Silver line of sun's
reflection below backlit plane of ridge in left
corner, man on nose of white longboard dropping
into the wave's next section.

Tomato London
Geoffrey Gatza

Soft limes tremble above hunting cougars. The accelerator was on full and we flew directly towards the smell. Heirloom women were there. Not now, but at some point in the distant future. I recognize/smell her. I have had her before. She will be hen in my house. The nest I built with my sweat and mucus. It is a warm nest, good for eggs and long winters. Onwards.

We inhaled the scent. John was driving. This was his idea.

I was cleaning my mouth, or really I only said I was to make it seem like I had some reason to let the machine screen the call. Would I go out? Tonight? I know it's hard to find a third on a whim, and I didn't have much to do. I did have a bottle of green in the cupboard, I'm ready for just about anything. No he didn't have anyone in mind, but if I was up for a quick hunt then take anyone, he really said anyone.

Would I bring my bottle and be the third? I'd be the second, wouldn't I? I asked, knowing that I'd have to be third. I'm always the third.

So it didn't turn out to be just anyone. Not the fat one who did say yes. Not the one with the glasses either. I liked her but John thought she smelled off. I was half way to the sun when she caught my eye. John thought she was empty. I knew better.

Here's what I say: I smelled her about two cycles ago and she was ripe with rot. A deep red rot that grows only on the highest mountaintops of the east. I love that springtime touch and this was a full lacerating liquor. It wasn't blue but something deep violet. She wore an eye patch and one of her left arms was decorated with a flowing ribbon. It was high fashion decades ago/a mysterious stance. A hired killer from a comic book, all knives and no skirt.

John got past her wind but I was hooked. I'm fast like that.

I was at one of these parties when I was a kid. The music was hot and the sex was lacerating. This is when I first met John. We hit several of the same nests and had a similar scent, so it was a first-rate match. We scammed so many kinds of couples it was lucky we both came out uncontaminated.

Then there was the time we met up with the police. They made me a third. I didn't want to, but it was hard to say no. They caught us with a hot bolt and it was obvious what they wanted. Gave me a shackle and I was out of my mind for weeks.

I stopped hanging with John after that. He was trouble/ couldn't smell well. I could, but I still went along. It was always my fault.

The red skies were rolled into the unruffled morning. I pulled the cork on the green and I took a long pull. I dabbed a bit behind my ear and over my cheeks. I felt that I could float on angel blossoms. We pulled over and the steam billowed around us. The nightlife cleared a wide berth and we strode unflappable in the downtown neon. All took notice of us, how could they not? All the heirloom women heard our audacity.

I tipped my hat to all the other thirds that captured my eye.

John spotted her from his lamp post and jumped up it, singing, *Ciao Bella*. She turned in a glimmer. Her scented belly beamed at me and she headed straight over. She took my hand and began walking towards Red's Falafel stand. Made John pay for her platter and spoon fed me like a lover should. Tonight I was all hers.

John was second so she talked with him and petted my black head, then chopped up some rocks while John turned on the stereo. I'd been in the shelter two weeks ago and now look at me! A new nest, a real friend, and fresh rocks being churned. Let demons explode!

I hit the green again and began to caress her shell. She took another drag from her stick and purred. I could feel her wetness. Her pores seeped brown droplets.

191

She was an angel, my angel. I was hers. I was the third. John kissed her upper mouth while she sang a sweet melody. It was going to be alright. All of me melted into her folds. She shook me. My suit was getting tangled in her legs. I hate these things, but right now tradition and desire resembled each other. I was robin's egg blue.

John now twirled around in front of her. She smiled at his agility. She was really getting into this/liquid was now pouring out of her belly. He danced while she sang. I began to enter her. My suit fit in all the places it should and she responded with a gentle tug of her legs, eggs and jelly warm on my chest. I thought of mother, my nose filled with her smell. I let loose and spilled onto her back. Her shell glistened orange/just seeing her white folds open. She dipped her finger into the glass of green and painted trails on my face. Her eyes told me everything.

On my eleventh cycle, my father told me that there were two kinds of men in this world. The man I became I would choose by my actions. Don't be an aimless wanderer. Those who lack aim get eaten. He told me of his third, how his suit didn't fit him correctly, how that was one of the reasons we were so poor. Life is a series of choices, and if I had purpose in my hikes, all of life would, or could be, food.

"I've told you things about fish that I've never told anyone else. How to take pliers and pull the skin to separate the flesh. One quick pull is what it takes to do it right. If not, the filet will rip and then the whole thing will be worthless. If done right, there will be an underlying flavor of death in each mouthful."

I wanted to be a second like my father and his father before him, but I have never had the courage to believe in nothing. The drama and passion is always in our minds, but the energy spent is nothing but an encore to the sensual aroma of fresh meat. Thinking of the fields of tenderloins growing in the plains make my fangs salivate. An alarm clock sounded in the background. I was stuck to her now. I could still grind into her belly. She turned me over. John touched my face. He was beautiful in this light. I smelled potatoes.

N ot everyone still has a place from where they've come, so Martin tries to describe it to a city girl one summer evening, strolling together past heroic statues and the homeless camped out like picnickers on the grass of a park that's on the verge of turning bronze. The shouts of Spanish kids from the baseball diamond beyond the park lagoon reminds him of playing outfield for the hometown team by the floodlights of tractors and combines and an enormous, rising moon. At twilight you could see the seams of the moon more clearly than the seams of the ball. He can remember a home run sailing over your head into a cornfield, sending up a cloudburst of crows...

Later, heading back with her to his dingy flat past open bars, the smell of sweat and spilled beer dissolves into a childhood odor of fermentation: the sour, abandoned granaries by the railroad tracks where the single spark from a match might still explode. A gang of boys would go there to smoke the pungent, impotent, home-grown dope and sometimes, they said, to meet a certain girl. They never knew when she'd be there. Just before she appeared the whine of locusts became deafening and grasshoppers whirred through the shimmering air. The daylight moon suddenly grew near enough for them to see that it was filled with the reflection of their little fragment of the world, and then the gliding shadow of a hawk ignited an explosion of pigeons from the granary silos.

Bohemian Rhapsody
Daniel Nester

As if in my own benediction ceremony, I would lay out all of the Queen albums, flush next to each other, in order of release, on my bedroom floor. The 45s from each album would lay on top of them, in the lower right-hand corner, also in order of release, from bottom to top.

I would then stand in front of this, drinking a wine cooler, as if I were Noah or in the ten commandments movie, congratulating myself, clasping my arms behind my back, as if this was my ark, my own creation; that I had, as if through my sheer accumulation and arrangement of these objects, some part of creating them.

Actually, back then, I am sure that I thought I had created them, at least in the form of the configuration I was looking at, and the Bartles & Jaymes tasted sweet going down my throat, and with my room clean and vacuumed, I would lie on my bed, jerking off.

When your wife says she's leaving you do not object. You don't even let her know you're insulted—you've already foreseen the foreseeable, quaint as it sounds, and the business no longer shocks you. Politely, agreeably, you tell her to do as she pleases, watching the suitcases open and fill. You tell her to call when she can. Does she need any money? She says you shouldn't be so agreeable. You nod. You tend to agree.

In a world so rife with contention, why disagree? Some people you know—neighbors, in-laws, people you work with—home in on discord like heat-seeking missiles. They blast great holes in their lives, thriving on willful, blood-boiling chaos. This is not you—agreeable, peaceable you. Ready-made hardened opinion, you feel, goes quite against nature. It defies this earth we breathe and traverse on, which is fluid, they say, and constantly shifting, alive at the core.

Last year, before this business began, you saw your daughter committed. Foreseeable, foreseen. Your daughter, who wasn't ever quite "there" in the first place, thinks she's a cipher, that she is turning into the wind. Better that, of course, than a cave girl out of Ms. What's-her-name's novels, those books your daughter drank in to enter prehistory. When you visit you don't debate her absent identity. You agree to the terms. You offer your fatherly best as it were, fresh-shaved, patient, mildly heroic, compact and trim if a bit frayed at the edges; no need to let her know you're depressed. You bring her the weight of your affable nature, your humor, your unswerving desire to accept and agree, along with a snack of some kind, some candy, a bag of almonds or unsalted peanuts.

The visits increase once her mother is gone. Three, say, or four times a week. The house has grown strange, to be truthful, and you like to get out. Your once-agreeable furnishings, the sofas and tables you decided to keep, have taken on auras, gray hazy outlines, which tend to unsettle. The bedroom exudes a disagreeable air. You hang around late at the office, rearranging your files; you visit your daughter. You sit in cafés on the weekends skimming the paper, thinking, deciding which movie to see. At night you awaken sitting upright in bed, discussing strange things with your curtains.

One Sunday, at an outdoor café, a man sits down at your table. He's thirty years younger than you, wide-shouldered, black-haired, bucktoothed. A fading tattoo on his hand. You come here a lot, he declares—he says he's seen you before. You do, you agree; he probably has. You're fond of the scones, you tell him. You glance at the crumbs on your plate.

Your agreeability, alas, makes you the ideal listener. People seem to sense this right off. You have a compassionate face, a kind face, you have heard. Like a beacon, your face pulls people in, strangers out of accord with good fortune, survivors and talkers, victims of the shipwreck of living.

The man has led a colorful life, as they say. He is funny, almost. You hear of his days as a kid in a much larger city, of all the hitchhiking he did, how for years he zigzagged the country, shacking up here, camping out there, he and a spotted castrated dog, a dog with one eye and one ear, a dog he called Lucky. You hear about his most recent romance.

He entertains, you have to admit. His problems, so vivid and real, draw you away from your invented anxieties. You lean back and listen, agreeably nodding, sipping your tea.

So I blow into town, he says, fully into his story. I go up to the apartment and open the door, and guess what?

You raise your eyebrows in question, unable to guess.

My girlfriend's in there with Eddy, he says, this guy from downstairs.

Delicacy forbids you to ask what were they doing, what did he see. You wipe your mouth with your napkin. You look at your watch. The story's growing less and less pleasant; you're afraid for the girl; you don't really like speaking with strangers. You take a few bills from you wallet and lay them down on the table.

He asks if you're leaving, teeth extended out past his lip. You tell him your daughter is waiting. You've had a nice chat. He asks you which way you're headed. You tell him. He says he's going that way. You need to hear the rest of the story.

Down the block by your car he says to hand over your billfold. The billfold, he says. You feel the nudge of the gun at your kidney.

You are no crime-drama hero. You hand over the billfold, agreeing in full to his terms. He opens the wallet and scowls. You've never carried much cash on your person. Move up the street, he says—removing your bank card from its niche in the leather, tucking the gun in his pocket—we'll stop at the bank. You move up the sidewalk. Nervous, giddy, you ask what became of his girlfriend.

I forgave her, he says, hands in his pockets. Then she skipped out.

He slides your card in the slot at the bank. You stand side by side. He asks for your PIN, which you promptly reveal. He taps in the code.

Silence. The street seems strangely deserted. You ask if he's found a new girlfriend.

Shut up, he says. He stuffs the cash in his pocket. Story's over.

Half-joking, you ask if he'd mind if you kept the receipt.

Shut up, I said, he exclaims.

You begin to say that you're sorry—you don't quite shut up in time—and then the hand is out of the pocket, there's a blur of tattoo and you're down on your knees in the flowerbed, there among nasturtiums and lupine and poppies, reeling from the shock of the blow.

Don't be so shit-eating nice, he says, his shadow looming over like Neanderthal Man's. He says you remind him of Eddy, that two-faced adulterous creep. Lay flat on the ground now, he tells you. Don't move for five minutes. Down, if you ever want to get up.

You lie in the dirt on your belly, no hero, purely compliant. In a while you touch your scalp where he hit you, fearing there's blood; there isn't. Your're lucky. The soil, barky and damp, clings to your fingers and hair. Your eyelashes brush against flowers—poppies, you think. Petals as vibrant as holiday pumpkins.

How long is five minutes?

People step up to get money. You hear them push in their cards and tap on the keyboard. You feel the individual discomfort, the dismay they endure to see such a sight, outlandish, right here out in the open, a man flung down on the ground in broad daylight, mashing the orange and blue flowers.

It seems you've been here forever. You've been here in dreams, you believe, in piecemeal visions—even this was foreseen in a way, if not quite clearly foreseeable. You should get up, you suppose, but you feel fine where you are. Sprawling, face in the black fragrant mulch, burrowing, digging in with your fingers, digging in like the wind. You press into the earth. The street grows quiet again. Ear to the ground, you hear plates trembling beneath you, weighty, incomprehensibly huge, aching with age and repeated collision, compelled by what is to agree and agree and agree.

The Porous Umbrella
Christopher Kennedy

When it rains, I grab my porous umbrella and
stand outside on the street. I stroll along with all
the others, our umbrellas raised over our heads
until the street becomes a garden of damp black flowers.
I love the feel of water as it filters through the tiny holes
and lands on my shoulders. And I know how to project the
appearance of a man, who knows exactly what to do when
the sky opens up above his head and the heavens send a
replenishing downpour.

I highly recommend you buy your own. Unless you're the
reckless type with no regard for how you're perceived.
Then I suggest you stand in the rain and be thought a
fool or follow the herd with their intact parasols, while
I create the illusion that I'm dry. But I say join me in my
surreptitious drench, and I'll teach you the secret of my
holey shoes.

The Order I Remember Our Roadside Reunion In
Jeff Parker

I realized it was pretty dark to be trotting through a wooded median between a divided highway, just as my feet slid in the wet leaves and I landed flat on my back, knocking my breath out and pinching something near my thighs. It was starting to rain. Spread eagle in the wet leaves, I lifted my head and noticed a stick poking up between my legs.

I was on the way to a wedding—my ex-girlfriend to my ex-best friend—when my Honda kicked it on I-23, a divided highway, which presented a choice: I could hitch on the side continuing toward the wedding, or I could make the short trek through the woods and look for help going the other way.

"Is that you?" she said.
"I have a stick through my scrotum," I said.
Her eyes fell to my crotch where the stick pointed back at her.
"Sharper than I remember it," she said.
"We're not the same mammal," I said.

As I trotted through the little wooded area to the other side of the divided highway, I wondered why it is that "girlfriend" gets to be one word while "best friend" is two? Aren't they basically the same animal? If I were going there, that's what I'd call them: Same Animal. Hi, Same Animal. Ah, Same Animal. My little fucking philosopher, turning to him. My darling anthropologist, turning to her.

The way something like this plays out: The word kindling pops into your head and you feel the wet of the wet leaves soaking through to your back. You reach for the stick to move it, it resists, you feel a foreign tug on yourself that is weird, you attempt to roll the stick between your fingertips and notice it's coming through the thin fabric of your wedding slacks, suddenly dawning on you, to your horror, that it is not *only* through the thin fabric of your wedding slacks.

I stood and bolted into the westbound lanes, hopping and flagging and screaming the word "kindling", and cars roared around me. The rain was really coming on.

When a car stopped, it was driven by some kind of white ghost, but once I opened the door I saw that it was my ex-girlfriend in her wedding dress and veil. She was wet too.

Soft Touch
Arielle Greenberg

He once got hit by a playground and it was all over for him with pockets. He couldn't eat breakfast for all the empty spaces. Holes distracted him. It was "as a child." But he wandered like a blank, sputtered, lost it.

The mind is a soft substance, a kind of pudding. Two million people have it, and it's caused by things we think are fun. By entertainment. Everyone has been touched by it in some way. Soft touch.

When we married and I sat with him in a park or office, he would want to call me at home. "I want to call Cathy." And I would say, "But I am Cathy. I'm here. I'm your wife." And he'd say, swingset, "I know you are, but I want to call the *other* Cathy." And so later at home there'd be a recording of his voice on the machine: "I just wondered what you were doing right now." A machine. A recording.

Was the other Cathy living in our house like a sock, like a closet, a shadow, a snake? Was I another Cathy? She became a palatable oatmeal on my tongue, on his. Me. The other Cathy. The other wife. The one he'd call when I was right by him.

"Is the other Cathy like me?" I asked him. "Oh, no," he said. "You're a lot easier to talk to." And I felt a little bad for Cathy then. The other me. But I had been the one feeding him out of my enormous pockets. My big white blouse. The other Cathy was just the hole in his morning meal, a fruit you open.

People get impacted by a game or a junglegym or some other form of violence and when they wander away I see them. I guess they could be more angry, suddenly very sweet, or afraid of bridges. In love with a thing they never knew before. A slight shift is all it takes.

Same Game
Anthony Tognazzini

E very day at the bus stop I see this little kid, about eight years old, hooded sweatshirt and white Nikes, bouncing a blue racquetball against the stippled asphalt.

"Catch," she said yesterday, and threw the ball in my direction.

Its rubber surface felt strange in my fingers, like a piece of fruit I didn't know the name of. It was still pretty early in the morning, and a heavy cloud cover hung low on the buildings. Everything looked like a shadow of itself. I'd seen this kid the day before, and the day before that, and she never seemed to be going anywhere, not school or camp or someone's house. She scared me. Her face was like a slate where you could scribble new expressions.

Finally, she said, "You look sad. Where are you going?"

"To work," I told her. "Everyday I take the bus, same time. See my briefcase? It's an adult thing. When you grow up, you'll see. It's not sad. You ride the bus, work, come home at night. Like that." I tossed the ball back. "You?" I asked. "Where're you going?"

The built-in reflector on the girl's sneaker gleamed. She said, "I'm going to be brave in ways you won't recognize." Then she pocketed her racquetball and ran away from me.

Paris: A Brief Descriptive Catalogue (from *The Paris Stories*)
Laird Hunt

> *De cent membres et visages qu'a chaque chose, j'en prens*
> *un... J'y donne une poincte, non pas plus largement, mais*
> *le plus profondement que je sçay... Sans dessein, sans*
> *promesse, je ne suis pas tenu d'en faire bon, ny de m'y*
> *tenir moy mesme, sans varier quand il me plaist, et me*
> *rendre au doubte et a l'incertitude, et a ma maitresse forme*
> *qui est l'ignorance.*
>
> —Michel de Montaigne

I

Dear Sweetheart,

On a sunny day in Paris you can observe shadows engaged in all shape and variety of exotica. Example: two long shadows, in the center of an immense and imbricate field of waving shadows, on either side of one short, squat, fixed shadow, unwrapping what you then look up and see are ice cream cones.

II

In 14th century Occitan (as reported by Jacques Fournier, Bishop of Pames, future Pope at Avignon), in a village called Montaillou, the 250 odd citizens (or heretics as Fournier had—too often literally—branded them) lived in envelopes of perceived space and time so small that by closing their eyes and making cross bars of their arms they could slip straight out of the spacio-temporal and finger the Divine.

This Divine, as most immediately if perhaps inaccurately personified by Fournier and his hot-poker and yellow-badge wielding Inquisition, was both ticklish and ill-tempered.

One swung one's arms carefully and guarded against the

incipient iniquity of closing one's eyes.

III

Years ago, before Paris, before this Paris, mine, I sat in a dark
room with 10 or 12 others and watched as an old projector
poured light onto a screen.

That was Physics.

Hands spilled liquids from glass to glass and we saw
viscosity.
Water rushed through turbines and cities turned on.
There was the dark granite steeple.
And there was the star.
The star's name was The Sun.

IV

I walked through the Musee de L'homme stopping here
in front of the Instruments of the World Display, and then
here in front of the Skull Display (4 grey skulls sitting on a
shelf), then here in front of the Overpopulation of the World
Display, and then here in the center of the Bridge of Infinity
Display where I opened my arms.
Which didn't accomplish much.
Once I asked a very small kid friend I had what she thought
happened to her skeleton when she slept, and her answer
was: Gravity.

Cars go by in the distance.
Everything goes by in the distance.

There is this anecdote I'm very much attached to about the
trip Flaubert took to North Africa with Maxime du Camp
in which Du Camp spent the whole trip trying out his new-
fangled photographic apparatus and Flaubert spent the
whole time dozing on the boat.

I repeat: I sleep too much.

Once a friend, albeit politely, complained about it. She said that maybe the next day, given it was Paris, and reportedly lovely, we could spend outside. I said something half-baked about the necessity of elaborating my relationship to the Orphic underworld.
She said that maybe the next day she would spend outside.

V

I associate, rightly or wrongly, my impending dissolution, with the dissolution, in my body, of time.

In this section of the Catalogue leaves beat against the window glass and I don't sleep.

Dear Sweetheart,

VI

In writing on medieval culture J. Le Goff speaks of an 'immense appetite for the Divine'. In going through my writings I came across this:

My Father illustrating the mechanisms of orbit.
His fist, Sun. A plum, Earth.
—And what about the Moon?
Fist. Plum. Fist.
We rose.
I understood the connective forces to be filament.
Clear.
—Like fishing line.
I could see it.
My fist shook.

Which runs, in combination with Le Goff's descriptive axiom, as a useful tangent to the following which I once (and you can believe I was jealous) overheard a young woman whispering to a young man on the metro:

"I wish I could kiss your bones."

VII

In THE HOURS OF CATHERINE OF CLEVES, a 14th century illuminated devotional, you can find a picture of Adam's bones lying in a tiny white pile at the base of a tree.

Dear Adam.

Orpheus had only his voice and lyre and walked almost out of hell with a jeweled shadow. Flaubert had only his pen and dozings and walked out of the 19th century with Paris. I walked out of my apartment and it was late Spring. Water was running in the gutters. People were sitting on the terraces. Someone, somewhere, was playing music. Couples were walking together along the street. I said something about the light playing off the water and onto the wall and a guy, some old guy I'd never seen before, stopped.
Yeah? he said.
I pointed.
He said, shhh. And walked off.

VIII

There is a commercial running on the movie screens of Paris that shows an elephant swimming through blue water. The blue water is in a bay surrounded by white cliffs and in the center of the bay is a young woman reading on a raft under a yellow umbrella beside two bottles of Coca Cola on ice. The elephant is filmed from the side then from below. The elephant is swimming towards the raft. The woman is very tan and everything outside the water with the exception of the Coca Cola on ice looks hot. There is lazy-summer-day music playing so we know that the goal of the elephant swimming towards the raft is a happy one. It is not possible to see what book the woman is reading though it's almost possible—for about half a second—to see her eyes. It is possible however to see the elephant's trunk: long, sinuous, strangely delicate, wet. The trunk silently deposits three water soaked peanuts on the raft then wraps itself around one of the bottles of Coke. Then the elephant swims off and music, woman, raft, blue water, white cliffs, yellow umbrella, Coke, ice, and elephant fade.

In THE DAY THE EARTH STOOD STILL the earth does not really stand still but for half an hour all engines and electricity stop. The people, however, do not stop, and for a moment, as I sat in the theater and watched them move through the maze of frozen cars, darkened hallways, and silenced streets, I was awed.

Joyce called Paris "The last of the human cities."

On a slim white column in "The last of the human cities." a young woman once projected the image of a hand pulling a stick through sand. I dreamed about it afterwards and in the dream the glowing hand moving around and around the column was moving around and around my finger.

I was in a bay once although the water was green not blue and it was cold and I was lost in it because my Father's arms hadn't reached me yet.

IX

One of a million medieval bright ideas was that the air was made of invisible wings.

It is fairly simple to make your arms into a representation of the crossbar. It is even simpler to close your eyes.

I opened them.

In this section of the Catalogue the leaves beat against the glass, the air is empty, and you are gone.

Sponde, in his love sonnets, writes endlessly on his indefatigable imperative: patience.

But though I lay down, hoping, too often to admit; too often, lately, I am tired.

X

These days, typically, the old projector pours its light, and on the screen there is nothing, so I write to you with my fingers all over the page:

Dear Sweetheart,

Paris is lovely the old labors are finished and I am outside standing in the sun.

Christine
Tony Leuzzi

Before she went to sleep, she crushed a spider with her thumb. In the morning, countless daddy long legs sprawled across her blanket.

And so she lost her virginity.

All day, men's hands brushed lightly at her skirt like loose leaves in the wind. In her dreams, those hands grew from the branches of twisting trees.

Visit to Her Husband
Lydia Davis

She and her husband are so nervous that throughout their conversation they keep going into the bathroom, closing the door, and using the toilet. Then they come out and light a cigarette. He goes in and urinates and leaves the toilet seat up and she goes in and lowers it and urinates. Toward the end of the afternoon, they stop talking about the divorce and start drinking. He drinks whiskey and she drinks beer. When it is time for her to go catch her train he has drunk a lot and goes into the bathroom one last time to urinate and doesn't bother to close the door.

As they are getting ready to go out, she begins to tell him the story of how she met her lover. While she is talking, he discovers that he has lost one of his expensive gloves and he is immediately upset and distracted. He leaves her to go look for his glove downstairs. Her story is half finished and he does not find his glove. He is less interested in her story when he comes back into the room without having found his glove. Later when they are walking together on the street he tells her happily how he has bought his girlfriend shoes for eighty dollars because he loves her so much.

When she is alone again, she is so preoccupied by what has taken place during the visit with her husband that she walks through the streets very quickly and bumps into several people in the subway and the train station. She has not even seen them but has come down on them like some natural element so suddenly that they did not have time to avoid her and she was surprised they were there at all. Some of these people look after her and say "Christ!"

In her parents' kitchen later she tries to explain something difficult about the divorce to her father and is angry when he doesn't understand, and then finds at the end of the explanation that she is eating an orange though she can't remember peeling it or even having decided to eat it.

Nine November
Sally Keith

Not I. Not sinking. But light. Light in town. The town in a valley, moreover, not sinking. Light in the alley. Because I looked. The alley not exactly sinking. More like arches, in fact. Framed in trees. Light bulbs light nodes and give blue light. Blue lights do not sink because I looked. Nor soak. Blue splays. Corroborate-blue. Splay on top of the tin roofs. Leaves scatter on tin roofs not catching light and not illuminated. Dark shapes. Tonight there is no wind.

Leaves lie on flat tin roofs and light stops there.

Yards lining the alley are fenced in strips. No. Fences are chain link. A clothesline divides one strip-yard into uneven parts. On the clothesline a woven rug. Because I looked. Light slides there. Because of light hitting a vine, climbing the fence closest to the alley, the leaf is shadowed on the weave. The shadow won't sink. The shadow is thrown and still. The night inside the alley is spots of separate light. Small stages.

A watering can stands on a post at night.

Rain has made the tracks connecting two alleys soft. Tulips and a lily and a chrysanthemum in patches of white where the fabric otherwise is dark. Flowers are framed for me in cloth. No, not for me. The yellow lamp inside the house lit it. Where else are objects inside the dark? Objects and no not because of me. Not sinking, but resolution. The world is also at night. Someone is on arrival.

Someone, not I, not for me, nor to me, is and looks.

The Listener
Aimee Parkison

Behind the broken rails of the white fence, she moved, startling the deer. Near the cattails, she fed scraps to the dogs tied to the east wall near her sister's face at the window, sweet breath fogging smudged glass. Every spring, the pond encroached upon the house after the rains, deer drinking from its murky edge where paint flecks floated, breaking apart on bark, leaves, and bottles filled with air. Styrofoam clashed with embers in the wind's wake, the cup torn apart. The dogs swam under their leashes to chase bits of biscuit floating out the door to the water. Mayflies skimmed the surface and clung to the window screens. As she watched the wings' shadow cross her sister's face, she didn't have anything to say. Even when she left the house, she would not speak to her brother in words. From her sister to her mother to her father's sun-darkened hands, vases, coffee cups, sugar cubes, and teaspoons were dried and exchanged in silence. Watching the dogs at the window, she often became confused and used her mouth for the wrong reasons. Her teeth were like her hands, another way to grasp and carry necessary items from the rooms to the windows and back. Venturing out into the half-immersed porch to sit on the swing in sunlight, she let her feet move in and out of the pond water. Crouching low as she swung, she amused her sister inside, feeding the dogs bread from her mouth. They leapt up to her lips delicately as in a kiss. Their paws splashed back into the water as they carried the bread away, quickly so that the others wouldn't steal the crumbs. Fingers were a last resort. Her sister didn't trust them to touch faces as she trusted a mouth no longer used for speaking. Stumbling toward the window, she pressed her face against the screen to feel the mayflies lighting on her cheek. Sometimes her hands like the deer could be forgotten even by the ones who waited for their return.

213

Notes for the Novice Ventriloquist
Gerry LaFemina

9 5% of what the dummy says is right. This you should know; the dummy is the id, its expressionless mouth like a dash drawn right above its jaw. Astonishing. Try not to be surprised when its voice isn't what you practiced. The dummy understands the spotlight better than you do.

~

In the biz, we're called Vents. The dummies, characters. We hold conventions with workshops titled "Don't Die on Stage" and "Repairing and Caring for your Character" and "The Real Scoop on Kid Shows." Mitchell, Kentucky, is the Mecca of Ventriloquism. You must make a pilgrimage at least once together. The thousands of dummies there will ignore you, their heads swivelled 180 degrees. They will welcome your character as a prodigal.

~

Say hello, Dummy.
Fuck you.

~

You have to know your audience. There will be children in the crowd. Old people. Know-it-alls watching for your lips to move. At talent shows watch out for those who can make glasses of water sing and avoid magicians. Never let your dummy volunteer to be sawed in half. Remember: your character likes the spotlight and magicians are notoriously jealous.

~

This, also, you should know: never take your dummy out on a date with you. It will belittle you in front of her. It will be witty and make dazzling conversation. As usual, you'll be the straight man, your tongue left in a Windsor knot around your tonsils. And when he leaves with her, his wooden arm wrapped around her waist, you'll be alone with the bill. You will swear later you heard your dummy laughing, saw a smile curving his lipless mouth.

Victim
Pedro Ponce

The victim is not deaf to the soundtrack. She is not blind to the audience leering over popcorn cartons. She knows. As she unlocks her door and steps into the darkened kitchen, as she turns on the lights and shuffles through the day's mail (mostly bills she will never have to pay), she knows. She's about to Get It. She sets down her purse and makes her way to the bedroom.

She sheds her clothes, ignoring the scattered whistles coming from the theater seats. She covers herself in a short silk robe. The flimsy material is too slight for the weather where she lives, but she knows the rules. A sudden scraping sound gives her an excuse to look out into the middle distance at the eyes watching her. She cannot let them see her look. Whatever fear she feels can register only briefly, for as long as it takes her to realize that the scraping is just a tree branch pressed against her window. Later, there will be the shadow behind the shower curtain, the thrust of a knife through the belly, the slow sinking to the tiled floor. For now, she must arrange herself into a blank, doe-eyed calm. She steps out to the living room for a cigarette.

The soundtrack swells with tortured strings and computerized shrieks. She must sit through it all, just another night at home on the sofa. Her friends at the office are home, too, with husbands or boyfriends, or else out at the bars. She desperately wants a beer. But there is no time. She looks over her shoulder and parts the curtains behind her. Beyond the frame, where the audience can't see, the paramedics have already arrived. A police car idles beside the ambulance. She sees the detective inside yawning as he waits for the screams that will signal his entrance.

She turns back to the dimly lit living room with what the audience takes to be a bemused stare. But she is actually looking squarely at the killer. He sullenly taps his watch while standing at the aquarium. The ridges of his clown mask are softened by the blue-green light of the tank. She takes one last drag on her cigarette and breathes it out in a narrow white funnel. Her satisfied smile is obscured as she vanishes down a darkened corridor.

The Postmodern Artist
Raymond Fedeman

One day he decided to paint on the walls of his studio everything that was inside the room. It was a large square room with a high ceiling and one window looking onto the street. First he reproduced the window on the wall opposite the window, so that now there was a perfect replica of the window, so realistically done that one could not tell which was the real window. Then he painted the paintings hanging on one wall, all of them self-portraits artfully framed, so that all the paintings of himself also appeared on the opposite wall but flattened into that wall, and yet just as well done and as convincingly as the originals. In one corner of the room a desk was standing against the wall. He painted the desk, and the chair in front of the desk, in the corner of the room directly opposite the real desk and chair. The composition and the perspective were so perfectly executed that if someone had entered the room and decided to sit at one of the desks, that person could not possibly have distinguished the real desk from its reproduction. On the ceiling he painted everything that stood on the floor, the working table, the chair, the paper basket, the easel, and himself too, but upside down of course, and yet so exactly replicated that someone standing on his head looking up at the ceiling could not possibly detect any difference between what stood on the floor and what was painted on the ceiling. Eventually all the objects in the studio were mirrored on the walls and on the ceiling, including the easel in the center of the room with the large canvas propped on it representing the room and the artist standing before the easel in the process of painting a portrait of himself. He then painted himself with a smile of satisfaction on his face standing before the easel in the painting of the easel he had reproduced on the wall. Finally he painted himself sitting at the imaginary desk, his head between his hands, elbows resting on top of the desk. For a while he stared at himself sitting at the imaginary desk, then he walked to the real desk, sat down, placed a large sheet of paper on the desk and began to sketch a picture of himself sitting at the desk sketching himself.

Shotgun Wedding in the Ribcage of the Bourgeoisie
Johannes Görannson

This time around I'll be more obscure, more unabashedly slashed in the backseat of the cab taking me back to the barn where I've tied Shirley Temple to a chair in an apparent homage to the tenderness of the charlatan class. The thrill is gone. All that remains are artistic movements and pig hoards trying to escape from my room. The rain comes down like hammers on infants. The parking lot stars know my story too well. They are trying to pick up the broken bottles before the immigrants come to exhibit their daughters in white gowns and plastic tiaras. Their long and slender fingers would be better suited to playing piano than picking splinters out of little girls' hair.

Put out your tongue
here.
No, it's not an ashtray.
It used to be
but now it's my heart.

"Why do you always have to ruin your poems with all this excess?" writes my former teacher who is teaching herself to death in the soggy Northwest. I'm just getting started photographing the pigs, using the same rope as I used for the immigrant children. Speaking of my damaged shell collection: My infatuations are becoming increasingly militaristic. Take Shirley. Just a few weeks ago I wouldn't have taught her Spanish without first removing the duct tape from her mouth. Take my torso. When I lived in New York I would never have used scissors. I would never have punctured the landscape painting without first painting the town with nail polish.

I must have fallen in love
with an arms manufacturer's daughter.
She got me a job as a gravedigger in the Bronx.
I fled town when I found out that the children were alive.

I hid a fist full of Christmas ornaments in her back.

The new disease is called *Joy*.

Too bad I'm suffering from the old disease, *Barnslighet*, which is spread through publicly sanctioned arson and press conferences.

My rabble-rousing has made me into something I can't get rid of. Gratuitous martyr. Vivisection hallucination. Lawn fires would be the logical conclusion but it's not the 20th century anymore. The kill shelter is not my torso anymore, it's a Greek chorus investigating my bleep anatomies. They let a dog into my room.

It stares at me. Sniffs at my knees.
I can barely see its eyes glimmer in the dark.
It whines like Shirley.
It walks away.

Rock n' roll must be dead. The tsar is coming back and now he wants what's his. My train tracks are high on his list. And so are my clang ribs. You should be worried, dear figure skater. Your name has been crossed out.

Satie's soundtrack for *Parade* is the only piece of classical music I've ever passed out to. Listen. Can you hear the Hispanic children playing it with their sticky fingers. The same keys over and over. On the pigs' eyes.

Caricature exercise:
That's not a pig.
That's a celebrity
according to the World War II
documentary I watched last night.
You can learn how to cut
like this
when you're finished
with the immigrant children.
Here's a tiara.

Watch out for the rusty nails.
That doesn't come until later.

Come back to my strangle. I want everything we do to involve gibberish anatomies. That's how best to transform our teenage milieu into something less freezing in the basement. Your skin looks lovely and milky tonight, Hypothermia. Your youth looks like the fake state flower of this hyperbole. I could do such offensive wonders with your mouth, but I won't. Not yet. There are enough parasites in this bed to make me royalty. King of Milk. Street of Thighs. I could make such a wonderful cake out of your face.

Before the academics can clean up my act
they have to figure out why my torso was sculptured
according to the neo-classical ideals of the Fall of Rome,
why the barbarians used kitchen knives.

We adapted Calvino's *Invisible Cities* because his mouth is full of soil. (Listen carefully: In the distance you can hear a door slam shut.)

My barn was built by a man who became famous for his caricatures of military leaders. He drew generals as pigs. He drew me as a punch in a model's mouth. He made me a paradise of fat girls. It is a political cartoon. I hang from the same gallows as Colin Powell. And all the pigs are wearing smiling monkey faces. I can't tell what the caption says. It's in German and smudged with what looks like a crushed mosquito. My caricaturist is gross. I'm full of puns and prickly utensils. He learned his compositional elegance from Dresden. He drew me as a roadblock. His passport worked as an illustration of the well-adjusted foreigner. My passport tells me to go home. I can't. My land is over. I can hear the applause through the wall.

The applause is dying down.
The audience is leaving.

I'm dancing with Shirley's ribbon in my mouth. My race

gestures offend animal rights activists. When the flashlight breaks I use my own hands on the model. She looks so much more colorful when I'm through with her. Fine. Leave. Last night was far more collided than this masturbation. Last night I was so far away I couldn't cut the pigs, couldn't even put out cigarettes on my ankles. Last night sounded like burning books but I can still read the first page. It's about immigrant children. It compares their insides to the gray insides of crawfish.

OK, so I'm not a novelist.
The buzzards think I'm a propagandist for meat.
The giggly girls think I glorify insects.
The saints can't understand
why the branches inside their clothes
break in the hours before dawn.

I'm eating pork tonight. I'm using it to bribe my model. I already gave her a camera. I gave it to her hard. I didn't do anything my brother didn't do to his apartment last night before blacking out. I wish he had saved the Replacements bootleg from Minneapolis, 1991. Since I went to that show, drunk on turpentine and laugh-track hysteria, fear has become my modus operandi. The hole in my head has become a salty flower.

The backlash has started to hurt the tourist industry.
My amnesia has made virginity self-referential.

There are plenty of prom queens to go around in this gymnasium but I want to make a brand new porno on this televised bombing of a chest. I'm starting to doubt the compositional elements of the epic. The witch-hunt metaphor doesn't work unless the reader has experienced transcendence. The fish bait is rotting in the swimming pool. The starvation exercises don't work without bourbon. The charlatan class cannot be burned without a more stupored mythology than my barn. I need to improve the locks. I can't finish the pigs. The countercreation has been co-opted by adoption agencies. What should I do with the residue on the balloon?

I need to paint my torso to look more like a torso and less like a jailbreak.

I keep mentioning my torso because I wish I were a zoologist. I wish I were a surgeon. Or Darwin. Or an ballet impresario in Paris. Or a mole in the ground. Or a reptile collector. Or 5000 accidents. Made of swans. Or Darwin. Or an injury. Or going home in a wheelbarrow. Or moving into the Hotel Fuck. Or bleeding slowly into a silver bucket. Or plundering. Most of all I wish I were Darwin.

Or 5000 accidents.

Made of swan feathers.

Marco Polo to Kublai Khan: My people will reduce all these marvelous cities to sugar in a toothless mouth.
The Khan: Are your people already that old?
Polo: No, we're infants. We speak in silhouettes.

OK, I speak in silhouettes and I do it with the zeal of a marching band but I'm sweating profusely in the sunshine and this plastic chair and my armpits and my chicken neck. If there were some snow in here the corridors wouldn't look so infected and the doctors wouldn't looked so rubbed. The teenagers would stop rubbing up against each other in the desks if someone had the guts to throw a brick through the window. There are no windows in this classroom unless something has changed since I last opened my eyes.

"Transcendence"

I use animals as props because they are made of meat.
I use the beautiful stars of track and field
because they won't make it
through the desert. I'm using this house
because it's not mine. I'm imitating
a divorce between the head and the heart

of a dissected eagle. I'm the son of a liar.
A fortunate son. My fortune is a burning barn.
My fortune says: Go home, burning child. I was born
on the border. On the other side: daguerreotype, winter.

(I erased the final paragraph because I don't want to be fired
and I don't want Ashcroft to throw me out of the country.
He cares so much about the youth of America, he would
never stand the neighing in my barn. That fucking pervert
loves to drink milk in the dark. I should know. I made him.
Nobody grows up in this torso. Nobody can act with duct-
tape over their mouth like our starlet can. The final scene:
trapped animals. Scratch. Scratch.)

Garker's Aestheticals

Brian Evenson

I.

It were a word. It name were God.

It gangled my tongue. It were crawed up my throat. Word God were given me the choke.

Spatted it out all about the crackwood floor. Luppen and lappen it up all from the crackwood floor. Gangled it trussed with my mean slivered tongue.

Pulped it pasty atween my molar teeth. Gave it the swallow, did I. Word went down smooth, did it. There were mouthwater to helpen it down. There were a swaller of nonesuch to helpen it down.

I frittered and setted about in some chairs. Stomach all gone achurn. Stomach were getten to got me up, given me the nudge for haven a spew. Took the spoon to the throat. Nothing come up. Looken way down my proper throat in the glass. Nothing done it to be sawn save the mean slivered tongue.

The guts on me wrought pain. It were fallen to the floor, for me. It were not gotten up, for me. Just the dry shake.

I shucked off the clothes.

I nuded there cold, shuddered in darkly.

II.

The sun were burnen the awful upsky course. The crackwood were all shite-ran to stank.

It were me the culprit. God were pointen the finger.

I scribed in my wastefuls upon floor, wall. I were thought to scribe upon my own bodywise, which I done. I sprent myself shitely.

III.

Night come on by. Men come on by. They getten their gander up with the most of it. They shored up the nostril for the stank.

Runnen the crackwood with shite were no proper etiquette, it were suggested me.

I weren't said none to answer.

They were got me by the limbses. I given nary a kick.

They pucked me up out of the miry bowel. I don't gatten no struggle still in me, don't done none with me. They went, carried me from the miry bowel.

But I were the last laugh, were I. I were it, I were. I were astank all to my way to my high heaven.

Kim Addonizio is the author, most recently, of the novel *Little Beauties* (Simon & Schuster). Her other books include *In the Box Called Pleasure*, stories (FC2); four poetry collections; and, with Dorianne Laux, *The Poet's Companion: A Guide to the Pleasures of Writing Poetry* (W.W. Norton).

Kazim Ali is the author of a novel, *Quinn's Passage*, and a book of poems, *The Far Mosque*. He is the publisher of Nightboat Books and assistant professor of English at Shippensburg University.

Dimitri Anastasopoulos's first novel, *A Larger Sense of Harvey*, was published by Mammoth Books. His second novel, *Life Preserver*, is about cosmetics, cannibalism, and alien visitations. He teaches at the University of Rochester.

Kenneth Bernard's latest book is *The Man in the Stretcher: Previously Uncollection Fiction* (Starcherone, 2005). Excerpts from his *Molloy Monologs* were performed last summer at the Lower East Side Festival of the Arts.

Eula Biss is the author of *The Balloonists*. Her essays have recently appeared in the *North American Review*, the *Massachusetts Review*, the *Bellingham Review,* and *Harper's*.

Nickole Brown graduated from the M.F.A. Program for Creative Writing at Vermont College. Her work has appeared in *The Cortland Review*, *Kestrel*, *The Writer's Chronicle*, *Poets & Writers*, and *Sudden Stories* (Mammoth Books). She also co-edited the anthology, *Air Fare: Stories, Poems, & Essays on Flight*. Nickole currently works at Sarabande Books in Louisville, Kentucky.

Brian Clements is the author of several collections of poetry in print and online, including *Essays Against Ruin, Burn Whatever Will Burn,* and *Flesh and Wood*. He is the editor of Firewheel Editions and of *Sentence: A Journal of Prose Poetics,* and he coordinates the MFA in Professional Writing at Western Connecticut State University.

Lydia Davis has been the author of numerous story collections over the past three decades; her most recent collection is *Samuel Johnson is Indignant* (Picador, 2002). Her honors include a Guggenheim Fellowship, a Lannan Foundation Award, a Wallace/Reader's Digest Award, a Chevalier from the French government, and a MacArthur grant. Her many translations include volumes by Michel Leiris, Maurice Blanchot, and Marcel Proust.

Sean Thomas Dougherty is the author of seven full-length books of prose and poems including the forthcoming *Broken Hallelujahs* (BOA Editions) and *Nightshift Belonging to Lorca* (Mammoth Books, 2004), a finalist for the 2005 Paterson Poetry Prize. He has also edited a critical book, *Maria Mazziotti Gillan* (Guernica Editions, 2006). His awards include a 2004 Pennsylvania Council for the Arts Fellowship in Poetry. He teaches all three genres in the BFA Program for Creative Writing at Penn State Erie.

Jamey Dunham's prose poems have appeared in *Paragraph, Sentence, Double Room, Great American Prose Poems: from Poe to the Present* (Scribner, 2003) and *The Best American Poetry 2005* (Scribner, 2005). He teaches at Sinclair Community College and lives in Cincinnati, Ohio, with his wife and children.

Stuart Dybek's most recent books are the novel-in-stories, *I Sailed with Magellan*, and a book of poetry, *Streets in their Own Ink*, both from FSG.

Brian Evenson is the director of the Literary Arts Program at Brown University. He has published more than a half dozen books of fiction, most recently *The Wavering Knife* (FC2).

Raymond Federman's new novel (his tenth) *The Farm* will be out later this year with FC2; the French version, under the title *Retour au Fumier*, came out in September 2005 with Les Editions Al Dante. Also in 2005, the stage adaptation of *Amer Eldorado* was performed 17 times at the Avignon Festival, and Federman appeared on stage for all of the performances.

Sherrie Flick's short-short fiction has appeared in numerous literary journals including *Prairie Schooner, North American Review, Quarterly West,* and *Quick Fiction.* In 2004, her chapbook, *I Call This Flirting,* won the Flume Press Fiction Award. She lives in Pittsburgh with her husband, the playwright Rick Schweikert.

Geoffrey Gatza has dedicated himself to protecting the downtrodden of his city from a continuing series of deadly poetic schemes by the insidious School of Quietude. He is editor and publisher of *BlazeVOX* Books. His web site is Geoffreygatza.com

Johannes Göransson was born in Sweden but has lived in the US for nearly 20 years. He is the co-founder and editor of Action Books, which published a selection of his translations of experimental Swedish poet Aase Berg in fall 2005.

Noah Eli Gordon is the author of *The Frequencies* (Tougher Disguises, 2003) and *The Area of Sound Called the Subtone* (Ahsahta Press, 2004), as well as numerous chapbooks, reviews, collaborations, and other itinerant writings.

Arielle Greenberg is the author of *My Kafka Century* (Action Books, 2005) and *Given* (Verse Press, 2002) and the chapbook *Fa(r)ther Down: Songs from the Allergy Trials* (New Michigan Press, 2003). She teaches at Columbia College Chicago and lives in Evanston with her family.

Joanna Howard's work has appeared in *Conjunctions, Chicago Review, Quarterly West, Western Humanities Review, Fourteen Hills,* and elsewhere. She is a fiction editor at *3rd bed*. She lives and works in Providence, RI.

Laird Hunt is the author of three novels, *The Impossibly, Indiana, Indiana,* and, most recently, *The Exquisite* (Coffee House Press, 2006). A former United Nations press officer, he currently teaches fiction and literature at the University of Denver.

Harold Jaffe is the author of nine volumes of fiction or "docufiction" and three novels. His work has been anthologized and translated into numerous languages, with his 1999 *Sex for the Millennium* released in France (Editions Denoel) in 2005. Jaffe is editor-in-chief of *Fiction International*.

Brian Johnson is the author of *Self-Portrait*. His work has appeared in *American Letters and Commentary, Quarter After Eight, The Styles,* and other journals.

Kent Johnson's latest book is *Lyric Poetry after Auschwitz: Eleven Submissions to the War* (Effing Press, 2005). His translation with Forrest Gander of Jaime Saenz's *The Night* is due out from Princeton University Press in 2006. He is a recent winner of NEA and PEN awards and was named State Teacher of the Year by the Illinois Community College Trustee's Association in 2004.

Sally Keith is the author of two collections of poetry, *Design* (Colorado Prize, University of Colorado, 2000) and *Dwelling Song* (University of Georgia, 2004). Her work has appeared in *Conjunctions, New American Writing, Volt, American Letters & Commentary,* and *Denver Quarterly,* among other journals. She is currently teaching at the University of Rochester.

Christopher Kennedy is the author of three full-length collections of poetry, *Nietzsche's Horse* (Mitki/Mitki Press), *Trouble with the Machine* (Low Fidelity Press), and *Encouragement for a Man Falling to His Death* (BOA Editions, Fall 2007) and three chapbooks, *Greatest Hits* (Pudding House), *King Cobra Does the Mambo* (M2 Press, forthcoming), and *"B" Sides* (M2 Press, forthcoming). He is the Director of the MFA Program in Creative Writing at Syracuse University and a founding editor of the literary journal, *3rd bed*.

Christine Boyka Kluge is the author of *Teaching Bones to Fly,* a poetry collection from Bitter Oleander Press, and *Domestic Weather,* which won the 2003 Uccelli Press Chapbook Contest. Her prose poetry and flash fiction collection, *Stirring the Mirror,* is due out from Bitter Oleander Press in 2007. Her writing is anthologized in *No Boundaries: Prose Poems by 24 American Poets, (Some from) Diagram, Sudden Stories,* and *Graphic Poetry.*

Gerry LaFemina is the author of *The Parakeets of Brooklyn, The Window Facing Winter,* and several other collections of poetry. He directs the Frostburg Center for Creative Writing at Frostburg

State University, and is co-editor of *Review Revue*, a journal of poetry reviews and prosody essays.

Tony Leuzzi teaches literature and composition at Monroe Community College in Rochester, NY. His poems and prose have appeared in a wide range of academic and small press journals and anthologies. A two-time recipient of writing-related grants from the New York State Council of the Arts, his book of verse, *Tongue-Tied and Singing*, was released by Foothills Press in 2004.

George Looney's third book, *The Precarious Rhetoric of Angels*, won the tenth annual White Pine Press Poetry Prize and was published in the fall of 2005. He directs the BFA in Creative Writing program at Penn State-Erie where he is editor-in-chief of *Lake Effect*, a national literary journal, and translation editor of *Mid-American Review*.

Gary Lutz is the author of *Stories in the Worst Way* (3rd bed Books) and *I Looked Alive* (Black Square Editions).

Peter Markus's most recent PP/FF book is *The Singing Fish* (Calamari Press). He is also the author of two other collections, *The Moon is a Lighthouse* (New Michigan Press) and *Good, Brother* (AWOL Press/Triple Press). His flash fictions/prose poems have appeared in recent issues of *Black Warrior Review, New Orleans Review, Massachusetts Review, 3rd bed, Quarterly West,* and *Willow Springs*.

Cris Mazza is the author of over a dozen novels and collections of fiction, including *Disability* and *Your Name Here: ___,* plus the critically acclaimed *Is It Sexual Harassment Yet?* and the PEN Nelson Algren Award winning *How to Leave a Country*. She is also author of a memoir, *Indigenous: Growing Up Californian,* and was co-editor of *Chick-Lit: Postfeminist Fiction* and *Chick-Lit 2 (No Chick Vics),* anthologies of alternative women's fiction.

Kathleen McGookey's work appears in the anthologies *The Party Train: A Collection of North American Prose Poetry* (New Rivers Press, 1995), *The Best of The Prose Poem: An International Journal* (White Pine Press, 2000), as well as in many literary magazines.

Her book, *Whatever Shines*, is available from White Pine Press, and her website is www.kathleenmcgookey.com.

Joyelle McSweeney is the author of *The Red Bird* and *The Commandrine and Other Poems*, both from Fence. She writes regular reviews for *The Constant Critic*, teaches at the University of Alabama and is the co-founder of Action Books, a press for poetry and translation.

Christina Milletti's collection, *The Religious and Other Fictions*, was published by Carnegie Mellon University Press in fall 2005. She teaches at the State University of New York at Buffalo.

Ander Monson lives in Michigan. He has published two books, *Other Electricities* (Sarabande Books, 2005), a novel, and *Vacationland* (Tupelo Press, 2005), a book of poetry.

Kirk Nesset's stories, poems and translations have appeared in *The Pushcart Prize Anthology, The Paris Review, Boston Review, Iowa Review, Witness,* and elsewhere. He is author of *Mr. Agreeable*, a book of short stories (Mammoth Press, forthcoming), and *The Stories of Raymond Carver*, a nonfiction study (Ohio University Press). He teaches creative writing and literature at Allegheny College.

Daniel Nester is the author of *God Save My Queen* (Soft Skull Press, 2003) and *God Save My Queen II* (Soft Skull Press, 2004). He is an assistant professor of English at The College of Saint Rose in Albany, NY.

Benjamin Paloff's poems have appeared in *The Antioch Review, The New Republic, The Paris Review,* and elsewhere. He is poetry co-editor of *Boston Review*.

Ethan Paquin's third book of poems, *The Violence*, was released in fall 2005 by Ahsahta Press. A native of New Hampshire, he lives and teaches in Buffalo, NY.

Jeff Parker's stories have appeared in *Ploughshares, Tin House, Another Chicago Magazine, Quick Fiction,* and in the anthologies

Life & Limb: Skateboarders Write from the Deep End (Soft Skull, 2004) and *Stumbling and Raging: More Political Fiction* (MacAdam / Cage, 2006).

Aimee Parkison teaches at UNC-Charlotte. She has won a Kurt Vonnegut Fiction Prize from *North American Review* and a Writers at Work fellowship, among other awards. *Woman with Dark Horses*, her debut collection of stories, won the first Starcherone Fiction Prize.

Ted Pelton is the author of three books, most recently the novel, *Malcolm & Jack (and Other Famous American Criminals)* (Spuyten Duyvil, 2006). Recipient of an NEA Fellowship for Fiction, he is an Associate Professor at Medaille College of Buffalo, NY, and Executive Director of Starcherone Books.

Pedro Ponce teaches fiction writing and 20th-Century American literature at St. Lawrence University. His short prose has previously appeared in *Quick Fiction, Double Room, DIAGRAM, Vestal Review,* and other publications.

Stephen Ratcliffe's latest books of poetry are *Portraits & Repetition* (The Post-Apollo Press, 2002) and *SOUND/(system)* (Green Integer, 2002). Recent poems have appeared in *1913, Bombay Gin, Common Knowledge, War & Peace, Conjunctions,* and *NO. Listening to Reading,* a book of essays on sound / shape and meaning in "experimental" poetry, was published by SUNY Press in 2000. He is the publisher of Avenue B and teaches at Mills College in Oakland.

Elizabeth Robinson is the author of six collections of poetry, most recently *Pure Descent,* a National Poetry Series winner, and *Apprehend,* winner of the Fence Modern Poets Prize. A new book, *Apostrophe,* is forthcoming from Apogee Press. She teaches at the University of Colorado in Boulder, and co-edits *26 Magazine,* Instance Press, and EtherDome Chapbooks.

Martha Ronk's most recent publications include *In a Landscape of Having to Repeat* (Omnidawn, 2004), which was winner of the 2005 PEN Center USA Literary Award for Poetry 2005, and *Why/ Why Not* (University of California Press, 2003). She was visiting writer-in-residence at the University of Colorado in June 2005 and is Irma and Jay Price Professor of English at Occidental College in Los Angeles.

Morgan Lucas Schuldt lectures at the University of Arizona where he also edits *CUE: A Journal of Prose Poetry*.

Daryl Scroggins lives with his wife in Dallas, where he works as a writer and a teacher. *The Game of Kings*, a book-length prose poem sequence, was published in 2001 by Rancho Loco Press, and *Winter Investments*, a collection of short stories, was published in 2003 by The Trilobite Press. *Prairie Shapes, a Flash Novel* won the 2004 Robert J. DeMott Prose Contest.

Nina Shope's debut collection, *Hangings: Three Novellas*, won the 2004-05 Starcherone Fiction Prize. A graduate of the MFA in Creative Writing program at Syracuse University, her fiction has appeared in *Open City*, *3rd bed*, and *Fourteen Hills*. She lives in Denver, Colorado.

Eleni Sikelianos's two new books are *The California Poem* (Coffee House) and *The Book of Jon* (Nonfiction; City Lights). Previous books include *The Monster Lives of Boys & Girls* (Green Integer, National Poetry Series), *Earliest Worlds* (Coffee House), and *The Book of Tendons* (Post-Apollo). She has received numerous awards for her poetry, nonfiction, and translations. She currently lives in Colorado.

Ed Taylor is a college instructor. His writing has appeared in *Fiction International*, *Another Chicago Magazine*, *Ontario Review*, *5_Trope*, *Slope*, and other print and online journals.

Anthony Tognazzini has published work in *Swink, The Hat, Sentence, Quarterly West, Salt Hill, La Petite Zine, The Mississippi Review, Quick Fiction, Ducky*, and *Hayden's Ferry Review*, among other journals, and in *Sudden Stories: A Mammoth Anthology of Miniscule Fiction*. He has received a Pushcart nomination and an award from the Academy of American Poets. He lives in Brooklyn, New York.

Alison Townsend is the author of two poetry collections, *The Blue Dress* and *What the Body Knows*, and her poetry and creative nonfiction appear widely, in magazines such as *Crab Orchard Review, Fourth Genre, The North American Review, The Southern Review*, and *Water-Stone*. She is an Associate Professor of English at the University of Wisconsin-Whitewater and lives on four acres of oak and prairie savanna in the farm country outside Madison.

Jessica Treat is the author of two story collections, *Not a Chance* (FC2, 2000) and *A Robber in the House* (Coffee House Press, 1993), and is completing a third. Her stories and prose poems have appeared in numerous journals and anthologies. She is the recipient of a Connecticut Commission on the Arts Award.

Mark Tursi is one of the founders and editors of the literary journal *Double Room*, and he is an Assistant Professor at College Misericordia in Pennsylvania. He received his Ph.D. from the University of Denver and his MFA from Colorado State University.

G.C. Waldrep's book of poems are *Goldbeater's Skin* (Colorado Prize, 2003) and *Disclamor* (BOA Editions, 2007). "What is a Hexachord" comes from a new manuscript, *Archicembalo*.

Thom Ward is the author of four poetry collections. He lives with his wife, three children, two dogs, two fish, and a rat in Penfield, New York.

Derek White is a writer, editor and publisher living in New York City. He operates Calamari Press and edits *SleepingFish* magazine. Short prose, art, and text/art of his have appeared in *Denver Quarterly, Post Road, Café Irreal, Diagram, Call Review, elimae*, and *Tarpaulin Sky*. "Capturing the Shadow Puppets" is from a forthcoming collection of dream-inspired flash fictions entitled *Poste Restante*.

Diane Williams's most recent book of fiction is *Romancer Erector*. She is the founding editor of the literary annual *Noon*.

Acknowledgments

"Testimony" and "But" by Kim Addonizio, reprinted from *In the Box Called Pleasure* © 1999 by Kim Addonizio. Reprinted by permission of FC2.

"Excerpt from *Quinn's Passage*" by Kazim Ali, reprinted from *Quinn's Passage* © 2005 by Kazim Ali. Reprinted by permission of BlazeVOX Books.

"Sister Francetta and the Pig Baby" by Kenneth Bernard is reprinted from *New American Review* with permission of the author.

"Prelude: The Box" by Eula Biss, reprinted from *The Balloonists* © 2002 by Eula Biss. Reprinted by permission of Hanging Loose Press.

"Apples the Eat Boy" by Brian Clements is reprinted from *Quick Fiction* with permission of the author.

"Visit To Her Husband" by Lydia Davis. Copyright © 1986 by Lydia Davis (New York: Farrar, Straus & Giroux, Inc.). "The Mother" by Lydia Davis. Copyright © 1986 by Lydia Davis (New York: Farrar, Straus & Giroux, Inc.). Both are reprinted by permission of the Denise Shannon Literary Agency, Inc.

"The Neighbor's Dog" by Jamey Dunham is reprinted from *Sentence* with permission of the author.

"Garker's Aestheticals" by Brian Evenson, reprinted from *The Wavering Knife* © 2004 by Brian Evenson. Reprinted by permission of FC2. "Story Barkers: A Report from the Field" by Brian Evenson is reprinted from *Unsaid* with permission of the author.

"This Is the Beginning of Time" by Sherrie Flick, reprinted from *I Call This Flirting* © 2004 Sherrie Flick. Reprinted by permission of Flume Press.

"The Laughing Alphabet" by Noah Eli Gordon is reprinted from *New American Writing* with permission of the author.

"The Black Cat" by Joanna Howard is reprinted from *Conjunctions* 42 with permission of the author.

"Paris: A Brief Descriptive Catalogue" by Laird Hunt is excerpted from *The Paris Stories* (Smokeproof Press, 2001) and is reprinted with permission of the author.

"Clown" by Harold Jaffe, reprinted from *15 Serial Killers* © 2003 by Harold Jaffe. Reproduced by permission of Raw Dog Screaming Press.

"Lyric Poetry After Auschwitz, or: 'Get the Hood Back On'" by Kent Johnson is reprinted from *Lyric Poetry after Auschwitz: Eleven Submissions to the War* © 2005 by Kent Johnson. Reprinted by permission of Effing Press. The poem first appeared in BlazeVOX.

"Falling Moon, Rising Stars" by Christine Boyka Kluge is reprinted from *Quarter After Eight*, where it appeared in slightly different form, with permission of the author.

"Fairytale" by Gerry LaFemina is reprinted from *Paradidomi Review* with permission of the author. "Notes for the Novice Ventriloquist" by Gerry LaFemina is reprinted from *Re-Divider* with permission of the author.

"Christine" by Tony Leuzzi is reprinted from *Double Room* with permission of the author.

"The Least Sneaky of Things" and "Uncle" by Gary Lutz, reprinted from *I Looked Alive* © 2004 by Gary Lutz. Reprinted by permission of Black Square Editions.

"We Make Mud" by Peter Markus is reprinted from *Another Chicago Magazine* with permission of the author.

"Araby" by Joyelle McSweeney is reprinted from *Sentence* with permission of the author.

"Big 32" by Ander Monson, reprinted from *Other Electricities* © 2005 by Ander Monson. Reprinted by permission of Sarabande Books.

"Bohemian Rhapsody" by Daniel Nester, reprinted from *God Save My Queen: A Tribute* by Daniel Nester © 2003 by Daniel Nester. Reprinted by permission of Soft Skull Press, Inc. www.softskull.com

"Mr. Agreeable" by Kirk Nesset is reprinted from *Fiction* and *Pushcart Prize Anthology XXIII* with permission of the author.

"The Order I Remember Our Roadside Reunion In" by Jeff Parker is reprinted from *Quick Fiction* with permission of the author.

"The Glass Girl" and "The Listener" by Aimee Parkison are reprinted from *Denver Quarterly* with permission of the author.

"Kitchen on Fire" by Ted Pelton is reprinted from *Endorsed by Jack Chapeau 2 an even*

PP/FF: an anthology

greater extent © 2006 by Ted Pelton. Reprinted by permission of Starcherone Books.

"Ladder" by Elizabeth Robinson is reprinted from *New Review of Literature* with permission of the author.

"Page 42" by Martha Ronk is reprinted from *The Harvard Review* with permission of the author.

"The Lightbulb" by Martha Ronk is reprinted from *American Letters & Commentary* with permission of the author.

"Triptych for Francis Bacon" by Morgan Lucas Schuldt is reprinted from *Sentence* with permission of the author.

Prairie Shapes, A Flash Novel by Daryl Scroggins is reprinted from *Quarter After Eight* with permission of the author.

"Date Unknown (Who is Talking/ Who is Remembering)" by Eleni Sikelianos, reprinted from *The Book of Jon* © 2004 by Eleni Sikelianos. Reprinted by permission of City Lights Books.

"Hunt Mountain" by Alison Townsend, reprinted from *The Blue Dress* © 2003 by Alison Townsend. Reprinted by permission of White Pine Press.

"Drive" by Jessica Treat is reprinted from *Double Room* with permission of the author.

"What is Hexachord" by G.C. Waldrep appeared first in *Web Conjunctions* and appears here by permission of the author.

"Capturing the Shadow Puppets" by Derek White is reprinted from *Snow Monkey* with permission of the author.

"The Source of Authority" by Diane Williams, reprinted from *Romancer Erector* © 2001 by Diane Williams. Reprinted by permission of Dalkey Archive Press.

About the Editor

Peter Conners is founding co-editor of the online literary journal, *Double Room: A Journal of Prose Poetry & Flash Fiction.* A collection of his poetry, *Of Whiskey and Winter,* will be published by White Pine Press in fall 2007. His writing appears regularly in such publications as *Fiction International, Sentence, Salt Hill, Quick Fiction, City Newspaper,* and, *American Book Review.* Two previous collections of his poetry and prose, *While in the World,* and *The Names of Winter,* were published by FootHills Publishing. Conners works as Marketing Director/Associate Editor for the poetry publisher BOA Editions. He lives with his wife and two sons in Rochester, NY.

Starcherone Books is an independent non-profit publisher of innovative fiction with dual commitments to discovering new writers and honoring recent avant-garde traditions.

The Blue of Her Body by Sara Greenslit (forthcoming, Fall 2006)
Beyond the Techno-Cave: A Guerrilla Writer's Guide to Post-Millennial Culture by Harold Jaffe (forthcoming, Fall 2006)
Peter: An (A)Historical Romance by Jeffrey DeShell
Endorsed by Jack Chapeau 2 an even greater extent (expanded 2nd ed.) by Ted Pelton
Hangings: Three Novellas by Nina Shope
My Body in Nine Parts by Raymond Federman
The Man in the Stretcher: Stories by Kenneth Bernard
Woman with Dark Horses: Stories by Aimee Parkison
Black Umbrella Stories by Nicolette de Csipkay
The Voice in the Closet by Raymond Federman

The deadline for our annual contest for new fiction is January 31. Queries are accepted during August and September.

Books can be purchased from our website, www.starcherone.com or through the mail at the address below. Our books are also available at finer bookstores or via Small Press Distribution, www.spdbooks.org.

Donations to Starcherone Books, a not-for-profit 501(c)(3) corporation, are tax deductible to the fullest extent permitted by law.

Write: Starcherone Books
                PO Box 303
                Buffalo, NY 14201-0303

Or visit: www.starcherone.com